LONELY PLANET
ROAD TRIP

LAKE MICHIGAN

Jim DuFresne

D1637422

MAY 1 8 2005

Road Trip Lake Michigan
1st edition – January 2005

Published by Lonely Planet Publications Pty Ltd
ABN 36 005 607 983

Australia	Head Office, Locked Bag 1, Footscray, Vic 3011
	☎ 03 8379 8000 fax 03 8379 8111
	🖥 talk2us@lonelyplanet.com.au
USA	150 Linden St, Oakland, CA 94607
	☎ 510 893 8555 toll free 800 275 8555
	fax 510 893 8572
	🖥 info@lonelyplanet.com
UK	72–82 Rosebery Avenue, London EC1R 4RW
	☎ 020 7841 9000 fax 020 7841 9001
	🖥 go@lonelyplanet.co.uk

This title was commissioned in Lonely Planet's Oakland office and produced by: **Commissioning Editor** & **Project Manager** Kathleen Munnelly **Series & Cover Designer** Candice Jacobus **Regional Publishing Manager** David Zingarelli

Freelancers: Cartographer Bart Wright **Layout Designer** Hayley Tsang **Editor** Wade Fox **Indexer** Ken DellaPenta **Proofer** Michele Posner

Cover photograph Lake Michigan shoreline, Holland Harbour, Richard Cummins/Lonely Planet Images. All images are copyright of the photographers unless otherwise indicated. This image is available for licensing from Lonely Planet Images:
🖥 www.lonelyplanetimages.com

ISBN 1 74059 938 1

Printed through The Bookmaker International Ltd. Printed in China

CONTENTS

FROM THE PUBLISHER

AUTHOR

Jim DuFresne

A lifelong resident of Michigan, Jim is the author of the Lonely Planet guidebooks *Tramping in New Zealand*, *Hiking in Alaska* and *Alaska*.

After spending a year studying and living in Chile and another in Mexico, my daughter returned home with an interest in working for Lonely Planet and asked if she could help with this book. I said sure and Jessica quickly learned two things. Travel writing is lot harder than it looks and Lake Michigan is more beautiful than she ever remembered.

In the end the real reward of this book for us was rediscovering Michigan's most remarkable region and working with Greg Hokans and Tim Putman of Mackinac Island, Peter Fritzsimmons and Diane Dakins of Petoskey, and Kelly Dunn of Traverse City. In particular we thank Patty Zwers of South Haven, Margaret Van Der Gracht of South Bend and most of all Kevin Hodgers for his outsider's insight on what makes Lake Michigan and its wonderful dunes so special.

SEND US YOUR FEEDBACK

We love to hear from travellers – your comments keep us on our toes and help make our books better. Our well-travelled team reads every word on what you loved or loathed about this book. Although we cannot reply individually to postal submissions, we always guarantee that your feedback goes straight to the appropriate authors, in time for the next edition – and the most useful submissions are rewarded with a free book. To send us your updates – and find out about LP events, newsletters and travel news – visit our award-winning website: 🖥 **www.lonelyplanet.com.**

Note: We may edit, reproduce and incorporate your comments in Lonely Planet products such as guidebooks, websites and digital products, so let us know if you don't want your comments reproduced or your name acknowledged. For a copy of our privacy policy visit 🖥 www.lonelyplanet.com/privacy.

HOW TO USE THIS BOOK

Opening hours for places listed in this book apply during summer, except where otherwise noted. When entry fees are not listed, sites are free (although some may request a small donation). Price gradings (eg $10/7/5) indicate admission for adults/students & seniors/children.

Text Symbols

☎	telephone	s	single rooms
🖥	internet available	d	double rooms
⊗	opening hours	ste	suites
Ⓟ	parking available	dm	dorm beds
🏊	swimming pool		

INTRODUCTION

Stroll the beach at Warren Dunes and you're just as likely to hear someone listening to a Chicago Cubs game on the radio as the Detroit Tigers, or reading the *Chicago Tribune* as the *Detroit Free Press*. Whose lakeshore is this?

Technically, the east shore of Lake Michigan is in the state of Michigan, but this special area has always been a popular destination for travelers throughout the Midwest, and particularly those from Chicago. And for good reasons: along Michigan's Gold Coast you have the world's largest collection of freshwater dunes, the best beaches in the Midwest and those glorious summer evenings when you can sit on the crest of a dune and watch the sun melt into the watery horizon.

Many say Lake Michigan tourism dates to 1871, the year of the Great Chicago Fire, which did more than just turn Mrs O'Leary's lantern-kicking cow into a platter of well-done steaks. A smoldering Chicago was rebuilt with Michigan white pine, the need for which created a string of mill towns along Lake Michigan, from Saugatuck and Pentwater to Manistee.

It was during those excursions to the sawmills that many discovered the sand, surf and sunsets of Lake Michigan. By the 1880s, the tourism boom was on, and it was fed by cities outside of Michigan – St Louis, South Bend and most of all Chicago. They arrived by steamships, then trains and finally automobiles, causing luxurious resorts to mushroom along the shoreline. When I-94 was completed in the early 1960s, it only cemented what was already a long and enduring relationship between the Windy City and the watery edge of Michigan. Many of Chicago's most famous residents have had cottages there, including the late Chicago mayor Richard M Daley, his son (the present mayor), Oprah Winfrey and George Wendt of the TV show *Cheers*.

This book covers a 465-mile road trip from Michiana, just north of the Indiana border, to Mackinac Island in Michigan's Upper Peninsula, an area often referred to as the Michigan Riviera. Keep in mind that the prices and hours listed here are for high season, Memorial Day through Labor Day. Tourism peaks from early July to late August, a time when it's difficult to obtain a room in many resorts or a campsite in a state park without reservations. If you plan to include the Windy City as part of your trip, pack along Lonely Planet's *Chicago* city guide.

GETTING THERE

Travelers driving from southeast Michigan or Toledo, Ohio take **I-75** and then **US 10**, **MI 72** or **MI 32** to reach the northern half of Lake Michigan and **I-94**, **I-96** and **I-196** to reach most of the southern half. Chicagoans and others coming from the west usually jump on **I-94** or the **Indiana Toll Road** (I-80/90) to **MI 39** or **US 31**. From Chicago/

Detroit it's a 120/180 mile drive to South Haven, 310/240 miles to Traverse City and 390/288 miles to Mackinaw City.

The main airports to access West Michigan are **Detroit Metropolitan Airport** (☎ 734-AIRPORT; www.metroairport.com) and **Chicago O'Hare** (☎ 773-686-2200; www.ohare.com), the world's busiest airport. Metro's main carrier is **Northwest Airlines** (☎ 800-447-4747; www. nwa.com). O'Hare is a hub for **United** (☎ 800-822-2746; www.ual. com) and **American Airlines** (☎ 800-433-7300; www.aa.com). Both airports have a glut of car rental companies including the biggies, **Avis** (☎ 800-230-4898; www.avis.com), **Budget** (☎ 800-527-0700; www.budget.com) and **Hertz** (☎ 800-654-3131; www.hertz.com).

By bus, **Greyhound** (☎ 800-229-9424; www.greyhound.com) connects a number of West Michigan cities, including Traverse City, South Haven, Petoskey and Holland, from both Chicago and Detroit. **Amtrak** (☎ 800-USA-RAIL; www.amtrak.com) has train departures from Chicago to Michigan City, St Joseph, Holland and Grand Rapids, but none directly to those cities from Detroit. You can also reach the Michigan shoreline from Wisconsin onboard two car ferries. The **SS Badger** (☎ 888-227-7447; www.ssbadger.com; roundtrip fare car/adult/child $98/78/36) sails between Manitowoc and Ludington. The **Lake Express LLC** (☎ 866-914-1010; www.lake-express.com; roundtrip fare car/adult/child $118/85/40) connects Milwaukee with Muskegon.

ITINERARIES

THE CLASSIC: ONE TO TWO WEEKS

If you can spare one to two weeks, there are two ways to vacation along Lake Michigan. You can slowly but steadily make your way up the coast, or you can plop down in one or two resort towns and split your time between day trips and long afternoons on the beach.

To explore the entire shoreline, begin with a couple of nights in **Douglas** or **Saugatuck**, stopping along the way to hike among the giant dunes at **Warren Dunes State Park** near Bridgman. Spend your second day exploring the art galleries and shops in Saugatuck or experiencing the Dutch culture of **Holland** just up the road. Head to **Manistee** for the next two days, stopping for a tour with Mac Wood's Dune Rides at **Silver Lake** and spending some time exploring Victorian **Manistee** and its many museums. Two more days should be devoted to either **Glen Arbor** or **Leland** to savor **Sleeping Bear Dunes National Lakeshore** and visit the vineyards of **Leelanau Peninsula**. Travel to **Petoskey** to see where Ernest Hemingway grew up, and look for Petoskey stones at **Fisherman's Island State Park**. If you have more time and any money left, spend a night on **Mackinac Island**.

Many travelers prefer using a town as a base and staying put. Three towns with a good range of motels, camping nearby and quick access to a variety of activities and sights are **Ludington**, **Traverse City** and **Mackinaw City**.

THE GREAT WEEKEND ESCAPE

Small quaint towns with historic inns, good restaurants, antique shops and, of course, great beaches make wonderful destinations for a weekend escape from the city. Here are some favorites, along with luxurious local inns that will pamper you. In **South Haven** (Carriage Inn) you can spend a day picking blueberries or visiting vineyards. Soak up the culture of **Saugatuck** (Wickwood Inn), home of numerous art and pottery galleries. At **Pentwater** (Nickerson Inn) you can spend a weekend learning to fly a kite at Charles Mears State Park or hiking the amazing dunes at Silver Lake State Park. **Harbor Springs** (Bay View Inn) has a quaint, small-town atmosphere but is only minutes from the great shopping, sunsets and nightlife of Petoskey.

HIGHLIGHTS

Warren Dunes State Park (p8): Climb towering dunes and walk more than two miles of beach.

Saugatuck (p14): Unwind in the B&B capital of Michigan, home to lots of art galleries, shops and an active gay community.

Mac Wood's Dunes Rides (p25): Jump in an open-air vehicle for a ride across the Silver Lake Dunes.

Big Sable Point Lighthouse (p26): Hike out to this remote lighthouse and then climb its tower for a stunning view of Lake Michigan.

Pierce Stocking Scenic Drive (p32): Enjoy the most impressive scenery in Sleeping Bear Dunes National Lakeshore along this 7.5-mile road.

Leland (p34): Explore the shops of Fishtown or dine at a restaurant in this trendy hamlet.

Old Mission Peninsula (p44): Spend an afternoon wine-tasting at local vineyards, and then purchase a bottle for sunset at the tip of the peninsula.

Fisherman's Island State Park (p46): Search for Petoskey stones, the ultimate souvenirs from Northern Michigan – there's no better place than here to find them.

Horton Bay General Store (p53): See where a youthful Ernest Hemingway spent his summers.

Mackinac Island (p58): Step back in time to when there were no cars on the roads, only horses and bicycles.

ON THE ROAD

From the Windy City, I-94 is a direct route to Harbor Country, and within 50 miles after leaving Illinois, you can be sitting on a beach in New Buffalo. For a more scenic, though slower, route, depart I-94 at Exit 11, head 2 miles north on I-69, then depart at Exit 261 and continue east along US 12. Within 2 miles, US 12 will begin skirting **Indiana Dunes National Lake Shore** and **Indiana Dunes State Park**.

The national lakeshore literally surrounds the state park, and together they preserve 15,000 acres and 14 miles of shoreline in a patchwork fashion. Oddly, at the west end of the parks is the massive US Steel foundry and, in the middle, Bethlehem Steel. Hey, this is Indiana, what do you expect? Keep on going to Michigan where they don't put steel mills next to the dunes.

For information or maps stop at the **Dorothy Buell Memorial Visitors Center** (☎ 219-926-7561; 1100 N Mineral Rd at Kemil Rd; ☼ 8am-6pm) in the lakeshore, the **state park headquarters** (☎ 219-926-1952; 1600 N 25 East; vehicle $8; ☼ 8:30am-4pm Mon-Fri) or the **Indiana Dunes State Park Nature Center** (☎ 219-926-1390; 1600 N 25 East; ☼ 10am-4pm Tue-Thu, 10am-5pm Fri-Sun). There is good hiking in the state park, which has 15 miles of trails along Lake Michigan and over dunes almost 200ft high. The best camping is at the state park **campground** (160 sites; modern/rustic $23/16) at the end of IN 49, an easy walk to Lake Michigan. The **Dunewood Campground** (☎ 219-874-2658; Broadway & US-12; site $15) in the lakeshore has 78 rustic sites, but it's a mile from the beach. The close proximity to Chicago makes these campgrounds and the beaches extremely popular. In short, they are jammed during the summer. From Indiana Dunes National Lakeshore you can stay on US 12 to reach Harbor Country.

HARBOR COUNTRY

Map 2

Stretching north for 20 miles from Indiana to Bridgman is Harbor Country, a string of small communities, golden beaches and numerous antique shops. Most Chicagoans can reach this delightful stretch of Lake Michigan in 90 minutes or less, making it a popular destination for a quick getaway.

Once you cross the state line on I-94 you can jump off. From Michigan City, head north on US 12 to immediately reach **Michiana** (pop 164) and in another 4 miles, **New Buffalo** (pop 2317), the largest of the towns. Continue on the Red Arrow Hwy after New Buffalo. Within 3 miles you'll pass through tiny **Union Pier**, and in another 10 miles is **Bridgman** (pop 2140). For more information contact the **Harbor Country Chamber of Commerce** (☎ 800-362-7251; www.harbor-country.org; 530 S Whittaker St, New Buffalo; ☼ 9am-5pm Mon-Fri, 10am-3pm Sat-Sun) in the New Buffalo Railroad Museum.

SIGHTS & ACTIVITIES

BEACHES

The prime attraction of this area is its beaches. Walking distance from downtown New Buffalo is the **New Buffalo Beach** (Whittaker St; vehicle $5). Even though it's next to a marina, the beach is protected from the wakes of the boats and is in a more natural setting than you would suspect. Near Bridgman is **Weko Beach** (☎ 269-465-5708; 9468 Red Arrow Hwy; vehicle $5), with more sugary sand, picnic facilities and observation decks on top of the dunes. The longest and best beach is at **Warren Dunes** (see **Warren Dunes State Park** below).

NEW BUFFALO RAILROAD MUSEUM
☎ 269-469-5409; 530 S Whittaker St, New Buffalo; admission free; ⊙ 9am-5pm Mon-Fri, 10am-3pm Sat-Sun

Housed in a replica of the original New Buffalo depot, this museum is devoted to the important role the railroad had in the town's development. Exhibits include a miniature train display and artifacts from the old depot.

TABOR HILL WINERY
☎ 800-283-3363; www.taborhill.com; 185 Mount Tabor Rd; tours free; ⊙ 12-4:30pm

The climate and soil along Lake Michigan lend themselves to wine cultivation, and there are a dozen vineyards between the shoreline and Paw Paw. To spend a day visiting them, pick up the *Southwest Michigan Wine Trail* at the Harbor Country Chamber of Commerce. One of the most scenic wineries is Tabor Hill, located among the rolling hills of Berrien County 8 miles from the Bridgman exit on I-94. You can tour the vineyard, sample the product in the tasting room or stay for dinner at Tabor Hill's excellent **restaurant** (mains $17-29; ⊙ 5-9:30pm Wed-Sat, 12-9pm Sun), where, in the summer, you can dine outdoors within view of the grapes. Reservations are recommended.

WARREN DUNES STATE PARK
☎ 269-426-4013; 12032 Red Arrow Hwy, Sawyer; vehicle resident/out-of-state $6/8

This is the first state park along Lake Michigan and one of the most popular. It draws more than a million visitors per year, and so many are from out of state that Warren Dunes is the only state park in Michigan that charges them a higher entry fee. The 200ft-high dunes are spectacular and so steep they are occasionally used by hang gliders. Most of this 1925-acre area is undeveloped and includes 2.5 miles of beautiful beach and 5 miles of trails through the dunes and along the shoreline. There are two campgrounds, a modern facility with 182 sites ($23) and a rustic one with 32 sites ($10). Be sure to reserve your **campsite** (reservations 800-44-PARKS; www.michigan.gov/dnr). The campgrounds are filled daily during the summer.

SLEEPING

GRAND BEACH MOTEL
☎ 269-469-1555; 19189 US 12, New Buffalo; d $50-70

Two miles southwest of New Buffalo, this family motel, with 14 simple but clean rooms and an outdoor pool, is one of the best deals in the area.

THE HARBOR GRAND
☎ 888-605-5900; www.harborgrand.com; 111 W Water St, New Buffalo; d $99-299, includes breakfast

With rooms overlooking Lake Michigan in downtown New Buffalo, the Harbor Grand has a relaxing atmosphere, bicycles for touring, a massage center and an indoor pool for when the lake is too cold.

INN AT UNION PIER
☎ 269-469-4700; www.innatunionpier.com; 9708 Berrien St, Union Pier; d $155-230

Nestled among trees and gardens, this inn is just across the road from Lake Michigan, only 200 steps from the beach, and has a wraparound porch, sauna, hot tub and 16 spacious rooms with private balconies and antique Swedish fireplaces. A gourmet breakfast is served in the morning, Michigan wines in the evening.

SNOOTY FOX
☎ 800-382-0836; 13416 Red Arrow Hwy, Harbert; cabins $85-95

The Snooty Fox is the place for those who want to experience the great outdoors but can't give up the luxury of a modern resort. Cabins are in private settings around a pond and are decorated with works by local artisans. The main lodge has Internet access, a library, kitchen facilities and a sauna.

EATING

HANNAH'S RESTAURANT
☎ 269-469-1440; 115 S Whittaker St, New Buffalo; mains $8-19; ⓧ 8am-10pm Sun-Thu, 8am-11pm Fri-Sat

This popular restaurant started out serving Bohemian dishes and now features a long and varied menu. You can still order old-world specialties, such as roast pork tenderloin served with homemade dumplings and scalloped apples. There is also a vegetarian menu.

PIERRE ANNE
☎ 269-469-9542; 9 S Buffalo St, New Buffalo; mains $7-10; ⓧ 11am-4pm Tue-Sun

A popular lunch destination, Pierre Anne serves soups, salads and its specialty, crepes. There are crepes for all tastes: sweet crepes, egg crepes, salmon crepes and even chicken teriyaki crepes.

RED ARROW ROADHOUSE
☎ 269-469-3939; 15710 Red Arrow Hwy; mains $10-18; ⓧ 5-10pm Mon-Thu, 12-11pm Fri-Sat, 12-10pm Sun

With a casual atmosphere and stuffed animals on the walls, this restaurant serves sandwiches, pastas and entrees such as ribs. Be sure to save room for the homemade pies and desserts.

HARBERT SWEDISH BAKERY & LUISA'S CAFÉ
☎ 269-469-9037; 13698 Red Arrow Hwy; mains $6-8; ⓧ café 7am-3pm, bakery 7am-6pm Thu-Mon

The bakery dates back to 1912, when Harbert's population was mainly Swedish. Today the bakery is a café that serves fresh soups, salads and excellent Mediterranean sandwiches but still bakes its traditional Swedish breads and cakes.

SHOPPING & ENTERTAINMENT

Harbor Country is an antique collector's paradise – Red Arrow Hwy is sprinkled with antique shops and malls. Two of the largest are the **Harbert Antique Mall** (☎ 269-469-0977; 13887 Red Arrow Hwy, Harbert; ☺ 10am-6pm Mon-Sat, 11am-6pm Sun) and **Lakeside Antiques** (☎ 269-469-4467; 14866 Red Arrow Hwy, Lakeside; ☺ 11am-6pm Mon-Sun).

You'll also find a cornucopia of fresh produce in this area. Along with seasonal fruit stands, there's **Jackson's Fruit Market** (☎ 269-469-4029; 2 E Buffalo St; ☺ 8am-9pm Mon-Sun Apr-Dec), which offers baskets of colorful flowers, plump watermelons and giant, vine-ripened tomatoes.

Shop 'til you drop for bargains at **Lighthouse Place Premium Outlets** (☎ 219-874-2915; 601 Wabash St, Michigan City; ☺ 9am-9pm Mon-Sat, 10am-6pm Sun), a sprawling complex with 120 national outlet stores just across the border in Indiana.

The **Dunes Summer Theatre** (☎ 219-879-7509; www.dunessummertheatre.com; 288 Shady Oaks Dr, Michiana Shores; tickets $15) stages a variety of plays and musicals throughout the summer. The **Woodworkers with the Blues** (☎ 269-469-5687; 13400 Red Arrow Hwy) is a day of music, storytelling and woodworking held at the end of June. At the beginning of August is the **Ship and Shore Festival** in New Buffalo, featuring food, beer tents, games, music and a lighted boat parade.

ON THE ROAD

From Bridgman, follow the Red Arrow Hwy north for 6.5 miles until it intersects with I-94 and Business I-94. Continue north on Business I-94, which, in 5 miles, swings through downtown **St Joseph**.

St Joseph (pop 9214) and **Benton Harbor** (pop 12,818) are sister cities with little in common. St Joseph has a mainly white, affluent population, while impoverished Benton Harbor, the home of Whirlpool appliances, is predominantly African American. Tensions have long been high between the two communities, separated by a short bridge but wide disparities.

St Joseph does have a long history of tourism and its upscale downtown is filled with shops, restaurants and several museums. For families, the entertaining **Curious Kids Museum** (☎ 269-983-2543; www.curiouskidsmuseum.org; 415 Lake Blvd; $5; ☺ 10am-5pm Mon-Sat, 12-5pm Sun) is worth a stop. This interactive museum has more than 100 exhibits that let kids try everything from picking apples and piloting a space shuttle to being a paleontologist and digging for dinosaur bones. The **Krasl Art Center** (☎ 269-983-0271; www.krasl.org; 707 Lake Blvd; admission free; ☺ 10am-4pm

Leave the beaches in Harbor Country for a quick side trip to small-town America. **Three Oaks** (pop 1786) is only 5 miles east of New Buffalo along US 12, yet many people drive much farther for the homemade sausages, hams and bologna at **Drier's Meat Market** (☎ 269-756-3101; 14 S Elm St; ☻ 9am-5pm Mon-Sat, 11am-5pm Sun). But it's not just the meat that makes this place special. Established in 1875, the shop is now a National Historic Site packed with antique meat grinders and faded photos of the old butchers. The **Vickers Theatre** (☎ 269-756-3522; www.vickerstheatre.com; 6 N Elm St; adults/students $8/6) is a restored vaudeville house offering an offbeat schedule of films – from classic French movies to current art films. Housed in the town's former railroad depot is the **Three Oaks Spokes Bicycle Museum** (☎ 269-756-3361; 1 Oak St; ☻ 9am-5pm Mon-Sun Mar-Dec), which exhibits antique bikes, some dating back to the 19th century. Rent bikes here and pick up a map to the museum's **Backroad Bikeways**, 12 routes that start at the depot and wind through the rural countryside along lightly used roads.

Mon-Thu & Sat, 10am-1pm Fri, 1-4pm Sun) has four galleries and a sculpture collection scattered throughout the museum grounds. For information on the area stop at the **Southwestern Michigan Tourist Council** (☎ 269-925-6301; www.swmichigan.org; 2300 Pipestone Rd; ☻ 8:30am-5pm Mon-Sat).

From Business I-94 in St Joseph, you can continue north on the Blue Star Hwy (MI 63), a scenic route to South Haven that's dotted with township parks and beaches. Within 8 miles is **Hager Park**, which has a playscape for young children and a wide beach for the rest of the family. **Van Buren State Park** (☎ 269-637-2788, 23960 Ruggles Rd; vehicle $6, site $19) is 18 miles from St Joseph. This 407-acre park is basically a large 220-site campground, a towering dune and a mile of wide Lake Michigan beach. Although it lacks hiking trails, both the campground and the beach are extremely popular during the summer. Make a **reservation** (☎ 800-44-PARKS; www.michigan.gov/dnr) if planning to camp. From the state park the Blue Star Hwy leads to South Haven in 4 miles.

SOUTH HAVEN

Population 5563; Map 5
The rambunctious boys of *American Pie 2* came here to party away a carefree summer. But even if your testosterone isn't raging, South Haven is an interesting place to visit. Located where the Black River flows into Lake Michigan, South Haven is wrapped around a lively marina and the weathered boats of a maritime museum, giving it the appearance of a coastal town in New England. Stop at the **South Haven Visitors Bureau** (☎ 269-637-5252, 800-SO-HAVEN; www.southhaven.org; 546 Phoenix St; ☻ 9am-5pm Mon-Thu, 9am-8pm

Fri, 10am-5pm Sat, 12-4pm Sun) for an armful of brochures and then spend a weekend here.

SIGHTS & ACTIVITIES

BEACHES
There are four public beaches downtown, and it's $5 to park at any of them. **Dyckman** (Dyckman Ave) and **Woodman Beach** (Woodman St) are both narrow and wedged between condos. Bordering the mouth of the Black River are **North Beach** (Lake Shore Dr) and **South Beach** (Jay R Monroe Blvd), with wider shorelines and piers on Lake Michigan. Grab a fishing pole and a bucket of minnows and join the anglers to see what's biting.

MICHIGAN MARITIME MUSEUM
☎ 269-637-8078, 800-747-3810; www.michiganmaritimemuseum.org; 260 Dyckman Ave; adult/child $2.50/1.50; ☷ 10am-5pm Mon-Sat, 12-5pm Sun
This interesting museum is dedicated to the boats that were built and used on the Great Lakes throughout history. Inside are vintage outboard motors and tools used by local shipbuilders. Outside is a boardwalk around a group of historical boats including the last wooden crafts used by the US Coast Guard.

U-PICK BLUEBERRIES
South Haven is the undisputed capital of Michigan's blueberry country. **DeGrandchamp's Blueberry Farm** (☎ 269-637-3915; 15575 77th St; ☷ 8am-6pm) and **Stephenson Farm** (☎ 269-637-4824; 6779 Baseline Rd; ☷ 9am-7pm) are great spots to pick your own. The South Haven Visitors Bureau has a list of all the fruit markets and 'U-pick' farms in this important fruit-producing region.

KAL-HAVEN TRAIL STATE PARK
☎ 269-637-2788; Blue Star Hwy & Wells St; individual/family $3/7; ☷ 8am-10pm
This rail trail starts in South Haven and runs 33 miles to Kalamazoo. Its gravel surface is ideal for hikers and mountain bikers. Among the places in South Haven to rent a bike is **Rock 'N Road Cycle** (☎ 269-639-0003; 315 Broadway; $15 a day; ☷ 10am-6pm Mon-Fri, 10am-4pm Sat).

SLEEPING & EATING

THE CARRIAGE HOUSE
☎ 269-639-2161; www.carriagehouseharbor.com; 118 Woodman; d $145-240
This exquisite B&B combines a Victorian summer-cottage atmosphere with modern luxuries such as in-room whirlpools.

OLD HARBOR INN
☎ 800-433-9210; www.oldharborinn.com; 515 Williams St; ste $119-299
On the first floor of this waterfront inn is York's Bar and Grill; on the second are 44 rooms and suites with private balconies or shared decks overlooking the harbor.

HOTEL NICHOLS

☎ 269-637-8725; www.hotelnichols.com; 201 Center St; d $100-180 includes breakfast

Built in 1878, this is the oldest hotel in South Haven and has 17 antique-furnished rooms downtown.

PHOENIX STREET CAFÉ

☎ 269-637-3600; 524 Phoenix St; mains $5-7; 7am-3pm

This family restaurant is downtown and will serve you a Greek omelet or lox and cream cheese for breakfast and homemade soups, vegetarian sandwiches or hamburgers for lunch.

THIRSTY PERCH WATERING HOLE & GRILL

☎ 269-639-8000; 272 Broadway St; mains $8-17; 11am-11pm Sun-Thu, 11am-12am Fri-Sat

The Thirsty Perch's long bar and multiple wide-screen TVs make it the ideal place for watching the Cubs lose another. Or, come just to dine on fish and chips, steaks, ribs or large salads.

THREE PELICANS

☎ 269-637-5123; 38 N Shore Dr; mains $10-30; 11:30am-11pm Sun-Thu, 11:30am-12am Fri-Sat

One of South Haven's finest restaurants, Three Pelicans has a maritime theme and outdoor seating overlooking the harbor. The menu is laden with seafood, such as chili-lime calamari, Thai coconut lobster and cilantro grilled salmon.

TELLO'S TRATTORIA

☎ 269-639-9898; 7379 N Shore Dr; mains $10-20; 11:30am-11pm Sun-Thu, 11:30pm-12am Fri-Sun

For Italian, locals head here for homemade pasta or signature dishes like *coniglio braseato*, rabbit braised in olive oil and served falling off the bone over risotto with a wild mushroom-wine sauce. The wine cellar is outstanding, and on the weekends there is live music and dancing in the Champagne Room.

SHOPPING & ENTERTAINMENT

Along Phoenix St are art galleries, gift shops and boutiques. For antiques, swing by **Murphy's Antique Mall** (☎ 269-639-1662; 321 Center St; 11am-6pm Mon & Wed-Sat, 1-6pm Sun), where you'll find two floors filled with everything from vintage jewelry and 1950s kitchenware to country furniture and 45rpm records and LPs. **The Blueberry Store** (☎ 269-637-6322; 525 Phoenix St; 10am-5:30pm Mon-Sat, 11am-4pm Sun) and its wide array of blueberry merchandise prove that the fruit can be used for more than just muffins.

Blueberry fanatics arrive in South Haven the second week of August for the **National Blueberry Festival** (www.blueberryfestival.com). The festival features a parade, a sand castle–building competition and everything that is blueberry. **Harborfest** in mid-June is three days of music, boat races and lighthouse tours. **The South Haven Center for the Arts** (☎ 269-637-1041; www.southhavenarts.org; 600 Phoenix St) offers performances that range from Brazilian jazz and Celtic music to 18th-century comic opera.

ON THE ROAD

It's a straight 17-mile shot from South Haven to Douglas along the Blue Star Hwy (County Rd A2). This route is much more interesting than I-196, passing several antique shops overflowing with yesterday's treasures (junk?). A good one is **Birdcage Antiques** (☎ 269-543-4732; 2378 Blue Star Hwy; 12-5pm), 14 miles north of South Haven. In between the antiques are a handful of art galleries and numerous farm stands selling just-picked fruit and vegetables during the summer. **The Blue Star Pottery** (☎ 269-637-5787; Blue Star Hwy; 11am-5pm Fri-Sun) is 2 miles north of South Haven and worth a quick stop.

In another 4 miles, turn right on 109th Ave to reach **Dutch Farm Market** (☎ 269-637-8334; 6067 109th Ave; 8am-7pm May-Nov) for homemade baked goods, jams, fresh pressed cider or, during the fall, a tour of the orchard in a horse-drawn wagon. The larger **Earl's Farm Market** (☎ 269-227-2074; 1630 Blue Star Hwy; 8am-8pm Jun-Oct) is 11 miles from South Haven and is where to pull over for raspberries, strawberries and blueberries when in season.

SAUGATUCK & DOUGLAS

Population: Douglas 1209, Saugatuck 1010; Map 2

Century-old homes, contemporary art galleries and chic boutiques make Saugatuck on Kalamazoo Lake a delightful destination – and

Saugatuck and Douglas' Gay Community

Beginning in the 1900s, Saugatuck established itself as an art colony and a town open to different lifestyles. It was such a refreshing change from West Michigan's ultra-religious and conservative bastions, such as Holland and Grand Rapids, that it immediately attracted gay and lesbian residents. The gay community has since greatly influenced the restaurants, shops and other businesses in both towns, and today Saugatuck is Michigan's most gay-friendly tourist destination. One notable hotspot is the **Dunes Resort** (☎ 269-857-1401; www.dunesresort.com; 333 Blue Star Hwy; d $60-150), which bills itself as Michigan's largest gay and lesbian resort complex and features a nightclub, cabaret and bistro bar. For a list of supportive businesses, including lodging, check out the website www.gaysaugatuckdouglas.com.

a very popular one during the summer, when at times it's almost impossible to find a parking spot.

Saugatuck's sister, Douglas, is not nearly as hip with shops and restaurants but is a good option for those who don't want to battle crowds. For information and brochures on the area, stop at the **Saugatuck/Douglas Convention and Visitors Bureau** (☎ 269-857-1701; www.saugatuck.com; 2902 Blue Star Hwy; 🕙 9am-5pm Mon-Fri).

SIGHTS & ACTIVITIES

BEACHES
Oval Beach (Oval Beach Rd; vehicle $5) is a beautiful stretch of sand on Lake Michigan and was rated one of the top five beaches in the US by MTV. You can drive to the beach or reach it on the **Saugatuck Chain Ferry** (☎ 269-857-4243; Water St; $1; 🕙 9am-9pm), which has been taking people across the Kalamazoo River since 1838. Once on the other side, follow a trail to the views at the top of Mount Baldhead, a 200ft-high dune, and then descend to Oval Beach.

For a more secluded swim, hike to Lake Michigan at **Saugatuck State Park** (☎ 269-637-2788; 64th St and 138th Ave; vehicle $6), 4 miles north of Saugatuck. The 1008-acre park has 2 miles of beach and 14 miles of trails that wind through forested and open dunes. The shortest trek to the lake is a mile.

ART WALKING TOUR
Scattered around both towns is **Art 'Round Town**, an outdoor exhibit of 40 contemporary sculptures. A dozen of the sculptures are permanent, but the rest rotate after judges choose them from entries submitted every fall. To locate all the sculptures, pick up an *ART Walking Tour* map from the visitors bureau.

SAUGATUCK DUNE RIDES
☎ 269-857-2253; www.saugatuckdunerides.com; 6495 Blue Star Hwy, Saugatuck; adult/child $14/9; 🕙 10am-7:30pm Mon-Sat, 11am-7:30pm Sun May-Sep

These blue dune buggies, with their funny, sometimes cheesy, tour guides, will take you for a half-hour ride through the dunes and woodlands of the Goshorn Lake Area. If you're planning on passing through Silver Lake, skip these and join the more interesting **Mac Wood's Dune Ride** (p25).

HARBOR DUCK ADVENTURES
☎ 269-857-3825; www.harborduck.com; Coughlin Park at Colver St, Saugatuck; adult/teen/child $15/10/5; 🕙 10am-7pm May-Sep

It's hard to miss this big, blue, half-boat-half-truck wheeling through town. The former WWII amphibious vessel has been turned into a 28-passenger wet taxi that offers a narrated tour of Saugatuck and Douglas and even crosses the Kalamazoo River between them. Passengers are free to leave the tour to shop and then board a later one.

STAR OF SAUGATUCK II

☎ 269-857-4261; www.saugatuckboatcruises.com; 716 Water St, Saugatuck; adult/child $13/7; ☽ 11am, 1pm, 3pm, 5pm & 8:15pm May-Oct

Designed to look like a Mississippi River paddleboat, the *Star of Saugatuck II* features 90-minute narrated tours that begin on the Kalamazoo River and end on Lake Michigan, including a sunset cruise at 8:15pm.

SS KEEWATIN MARITIME MUSEUM

☎ 269-857-2464; www.keewatinmaritimemuseum.com; 225 Union St, Douglas; adult/child $8/4; ☽ 10am-4:30pm Jun-Aug

A remnant of the golden era of steamship travel, this 350ft vessel offered passenger service on the Great Lakes until 1965. Now it's a maritime museum permanently moored in the Kalamazoo River just off Blue Star Hwy. The 45-minute guided tour leads you throughout the steamship and ends with the maritime exhibits housed on the lower deck.

SLEEPING

THE PINES MOTEL

☎ 269-857-5211; www.thepinesmotorlodge.com; 56 Blue Star Hwy, Douglas; d ☽ $115-165 includes breakfast

Tired of Victorian B&Bs? Then switch eras and check out this funky, retro motel that has recently been renovated with a 1950s flair. Rooms are clean and airy.

THE KIRBY HOUSE

☎ 800-521-6473; www.kirbyhouse.com; 294 W Center St, Saugatuck; d $115-175

A Michigan historic site, this B&B was built in 1890 and later served as a hospital for almost 30 years. Nestled among gardens, the Kirby House has a long, wraparound porch and heated pool. Every morning guests are treated to a gourmet breakfast by candlelight.

MAPLEWOOD HOTEL

☎ 269-857-1771; www.maplewoodhotel.com; 428 Butler St, Saugatuck; d $150-250 includes breakfast

Conveniently located downtown, this 15-room hotel is a stately white mansion built in the 1860s. Rooms are large with private baths and filled with antiques. Suites have Jacuzzis and fireplaces. During the summer, you can take a dip in the heated outdoor pool.

WICKWOOD INN

☎ 269-857-1465, 800-385-1174; www.wickwoodinn.com; 510 Butler St, Saugatuck; d $230-350

Truly a treat for the palate! Julee Rosso, the author of *The Silver Palate* cookbooks, now runs this charming, historic inn that serves a tempting brunch in the morning, tea and cookies in the afternoon and homemade brandy and brownies before you turn in.

EATING

EVERYDAY PEOPLE CAFÉ
☎ 269-857-4240; 11 Center, Douglas; mains $12-22; ⏲ lunch 11am-2pm Mon-Tue & Fri, dinner 5:30-10pm Sun-Tue & Thu, 5:30-11pm Fri-Sat

A hip café that you would expect to find in Saugatuck. The menu includes such dishes as chipotle barbecue pork sandwiches and stuffed portabella mushrooms along with soups and salads. In the backyard is a wine garden, and Sundays feature live music.

BLUE MOON BAR & GRILL
☎ 269-857-8686; 310 Blue Star Hwy, Douglas; mains $18-28; ⏲ 11am-11pm

With a modern interior and an outdoor patio, the Blue Moon offers an eclectic menu that includes blackberry duck salad and chilled poached salmon with cucumber-yogurt sauce.

THE LOAF AND MUG
☎ 269-857-3793; 236 Culver St, Saugatuck; mains $6.50-13; ⏲ 9am-9pm Wed-Sun, 9am-3pm Tue

The outside of this restaurant and bakery is Old World, while inside is cozy and filled with the aroma of just-baked bread and pastries. The Loaf and Mug serves sandwiches, breakfast dishes, soups and tapas such as chile-and-lime-marinated grouper and grilled asparagus on bruschetta.

MERMAID BAR & GRILL
☎ 269-857-8208; 360 Water St, Saugatuck; mains $7.50-18; ⏲ 11:30am-9:30pm Sun-Thu, 11:30am-11pm Fri-Sat

Featuring outdoor seating overlooking the harbor, this popular restaurant and bar serves up dishes ranging from burgers to pasta with shrimp and goat cheese.

RESTAURANT TOULOUSE
☎ 269-857-1561; 248 Culver St, Saugatuck; mains $14-28; ⏲ 5:30-9pm Mon-Fri, 5:30-10pm Sat-Sun

This upscale restaurant has a French-country theme and is surrounded by gardens. Favorite dishes include foie gras, cassoulet and coquilles St Jacques.

SHOPPING & ENTERTAINMENT

Both downtown areas, but especially Saugatuck's, have numerous art galleries and shops. In Saugatuck, the majority of galleries are around Water St and Butler St. Among the local artists with a studio and gallery are **Bruce Baughman** (☎ 269-857-1299; www.brucebaughmangallery.com; 242 Butler St, Saugatuck; ⏲ 11am-5pm) and **Lynn Neuman** (☎ 269-857-7262; 36 Center St, Douglas; ⏲ 10:30am-5pm Mon-Thu, 10:30am-9pm Fri-Sat), who specializes in watercolors and oils. Saugatuck is also loaded with interesting shops, particularly clothing stores. At **Vinyl Palette** (☎ 269-857-7664;

3383 Blue Star Hwy; ⊗ 11am-5:30pm Mon and Wed-Sat) you can still purchase 45rpm records and LPs. Unusual beach and resort wear can be found at **Bali Bali** (☎ 269-857-1678; 245 Butler St; ⊗ 11am-6pm).

Many restaurants offer entertainment, including **Phil's Bar & Grill** (☎ 269-857-1555; 215 Butler St, Saugatuck; ⊗ 11:30am-12am Mon-Sat, 12pm-12am Sun), a lively tavern at night. For live theater, there is the **Mason Street Warehouse** (☎ 269-857-4898; www.mason-streetwarehouse.org; 400 Culver St, Saugatuck; $27.50-30; ⊗ Jul-Sep), which stages musicals. Saugatuck's **Waterfront Film Festival** (www.waterfrontfilm.org), one of the few in Michigan, showcases small-budget, independent films for three days in mid-June.

HOLLAND

Population 25,086; Map 2

It's not quite Amsterdam, but Holland does have more than its share of tulips, wooden shoes and even a windmill. Founded by Dutch religious dissenters in 1847, Holland today is still the center of Dutch culture in Michigan and famous for its tulip festival in mid-May.

Holland is an interesting place to visit for the day, but lacks the charming resort atmosphere of a Charlevoix or Saugatuck. Lodging for the most part is limited to major chain motels. The **Holland Area Convention & Visitor's Bureau** (☎ 800-506-1299; www.holland. org; 76 E 8th St; ⊗ 8am-5pm Mon-Fri, 10:30am-3:30pm Sat) has information on the area.

SIGHTS & ACTIVITIES

WINDMILL ISLAND

☎ 616-355-1030; www.windmillisland.org; 1 Lincoln Ave; adult/child $6.50/3.50; ⊗ 9am-6pm Mon-Sat, 11:30am-6pm Sun Apr-Oct

This island is the center of Dutch culture in Holland and a colorful sight during tulip season, when it's literally covered by the vibrant flower. Other park attractions include *DeZwaan*, the country's only authentic Dutch windmill, Klompen dancers in bright costumes and wooden shoes, an Amsterdam street organ and a miniature Netherlands village.

DUTCH VILLAGE

☎ 616-396-1475; www.dutchvillage.com; 12350 James St; adult/child $8/5; ⊗ 9am-6pm

A Dutch theme park? You bet! Hokey to some, nostalgic to others, Dutch Village started out as a tulip farm before being transformed into a roadside attraction that tries to depict the life Holland's immigrants left behind in the 19th century. Along with a wooden shoe factory, Dutch folk dancing and elaborate street organs, there are rides, such as a wooden shoe slide, and, of course, plenty of gift shops.

THE HOLLAND PRINCESS
☎ 616-393-7799; www.hollandprincess.com; 290 Howard St; $14-44
This 65ft, Victorian-style riverboat cruises Lake Macatawa, offering trips that range from a 1½ hour history tour to a dinner cruise with live music.

MUSEUMS
There are two museums downtown that showcase Dutch life. **The Holland Museum** (☎ 888-200-9123; www.hollandmuseum.org; 31 W 10th St; $3; 🕙 10am-5pm Mon, Wed, Fri-Sat, 10am-8pm Thu, 2-5pm Sun), housed in the city's impressive former post office, traces the development of Holland and is renowned for its Delft pottery exhibit. **The Cappon House** (☎ 616-392-6740; 228 W 9th St; $3; 🕙 1-4pm Wed-Sat May-Oct) was built in 1874 by the Dutch immigrant Isaac Cappon. Today, you can tour the furnished home and learn Cappon's Cinderella story, how he came from rags to become one of Holland's most wealthy and influential leaders.

SLEEPING & EATING

HOLLAND STATE PARK
☎ 616-399-9390; 2215 Ottawa Beach Rd; sites $29
This 142-acre state park with its wide sandy beach is one of the most popular in Michigan, attracting more than two million visitors a year. The park has two campgrounds with 211 sites across the street from Lake Macatawa and 98 more adjacent to the day-use area on Lake Michigan. Make **reservations** (☎ 800-44-PARKS; www.michigan.gov/dnr) well in advance.

DUTCH COLONIAL INN
☎ 616-396-3664; www.dutchcolonialinn.com; 560 Central Ave; d $100-160
Covered in flower patterns, this home was built in the 1920s in a neighborhood close to the downtown area and is one of Holland's best B&Bs. The inn has four rooms, most with whirlpool tubs and fireplaces.

HOLIDAY INN EXPRESS
☎ 616-738-2800, 866-315-6182; 12381 Felch St; d $109-119 includes breakfast
This Easter egg–colored hotel is a fun place for kids, with a Michigan-shaped pool, a game room and an outdoor sports court.

NEW HOLLAND BREWING CO
☎ 616-355-6422; 66 E 8th St; mains $7-15; 🕙 11am-12am Sun-Thu, 11am-1am Fri-Sat
Wash down a pesto pizza or a hearty sandwich with one of their handcrafted beers. This brew pub produces pumpkin ale, stout and Paleooza, a smooth pale ale that is a local favorite.

BUTCH'S
☎ 616-396-8227; 44 E 8th St; mains $7-29; 🕙 10am-9:30pm Mon-Sat
Butch's is a large and lively deli with a bar and an upscale dinner

menu. At lunchtime you can choose from a variety of sandwiches made with homemade bread and imported cheeses and filled with such delectable treats as smoked duck breast and salmon.

ALPENROSE
☎ 616-393-2111; www.alpenroserestaurant.com; 4 E 8th St; mains $19-29; 🕑 11am-9pm Mon-Sat, 10am-2pm Sun

The AlpenRose serves Austrian and Continental cuisine from Wiener Schnitzel to chicken stuffed with sage, Derby cheese and caramelized mushrooms. The original owner came from Austria to work as a pastry chef at the Grand Hotel on Mackinac Island, and the restaurant has since maintained its excellent menu of desserts and pastries.

WINDMILL RESTAURANT
☎ 616-392-2726; 28 W 8th St; mains $4-7; 🕑 5am-4pm Mon-Sat, 7am-2pm Sun

The Windmill is a bustling diner that serves breakfast all day and such American dishes as meat loaf, hamburgers and fried chicken.

SHOPPING & ENTERTAINMENT

The century-old buildings that line 8th St make up Holland's main downtown shopping area, while north on US 31 is the **Holland Outlet Center** (☎ 616-396-1808; 12330 James St; 🕑 10am-8pm Mon-Sat, 11am-6pm Sun) housing discount stores for brands such as Gap and Reebok. Also right off of US 31 is the **Veldheer's Tulip Farm/DeKlomp Wooden Shoe and Delftware Factory** (☎ 616-399-1900; www.veldheer.com; 12755 Quincy St; 🕑 8am-6pm Mon-Fri, 9am-5pm Sat-Sun) where you can watch workers make wooden shoes or blue and white Delft pottery.

Tourists swarm the city for the renowned **Tulip Time Festival** at the beginning of May. For a week, the city blooms with millions of tulips, thousands of Klompen dancers, three parades, and countless numbers of wooden shoes clogging along the streets. There is a full-time **Tulip Time Festival Office** (☎ 800-822-2770; www.tuliptime.org; 171 Lincoln Ave) dedicated to planning and staging the massive event.

The **Holland Symphony Orchestra** (☎ 616-494-0256; www.hollandsymphony.org; 150 E 8th St) performs year-round in various venues throughout the city.

ON THE ROAD

Lake Shore Ave is the back-road alternative to US 31 from Holland to Grand Haven. Pick it up from Ottawa Beach Rd, just before entering Holland State Park on the north side of Lake Macatawa, and within minutes you are hugging Lake Michigan for most of the 22 miles to Grand Haven. The route is in Ottawa County, which maintains some of the best county parks in the state, including several along this stretch. Other than the parks, beachfront homes and a Consumers Power plant, this stretch is devoid of restaurants, hotels and other attractions.

Less than 2 miles along Lake Shore Ave is **Tunnel Park** (☎ 616-783-4810; 66 Lake Shore Ave; vehicles $5; ⏰ 7am-10pm May-Oct). True to its name, a tunnel walkway cuts through the middle of a huge dune and leads to the beach. There is also a dune climb to run down and sweeping views of Lake Michigan from a deck at the crest of the dune.

In another 10 miles is wonderful **Kirk Park** (☎ 616-783-4810; 9791 Lake Shore Ave; vehicles $5; ⏰ 7am-10pm), with 68 acres of wooded dunes, a wide beach on Lake Michigan and nature trails to more panoramic views of the Great Lake. Cyclists will also love Ottawa County, which maintains an extensive bike path system, including a path along Lake Shore Ave from Holland State Park to Grand Haven. All the bike paths are covered in *Western Ottawa County Bicycle Path Maps,* a brochure available at the visitors centers in Holland and Grand Haven.

GRAND HAVEN

Population 11,168; Map 6

Overshadowed by Muskegon and only a half-hour from Grand Rapids, this beach town is still one of the most popular in the state. The sand is great and the nights are lively; book summer weekend reservations as far in advance as you can. The **Grand Haven Chamber of Commerce** (☎ 800-303-4096; www.grandhavenchamber.org; 1 S Harbor Dr; ⏰ 8am-5pm Mon-Fri, 10am-2pm Sat) is well stocked with brochures.

SIGHTS & ACTIVITIES

BOARDWALK

Skirting the Grand River from the historic **Grand Haven Lighthouse** to **Chinook Pier**, this 2.5-mile pedestrian path is one of the best river walks in Michigan and is lined with benches, historical displays, ice-cream and hot-dog stands and a continuous view of the boat traffic heading out to Lake Michigan. Also on the Boardwalk is the **Tri-Cities Museum** (☎ 616-842-0700; www.grandhaven.com/museum; 1 N Harbor Dr; admission free; ⏰ 10am-9:30pm Tue-Sat, 12-9:30pm Sun). Housed in the former Grand Trunk Railroad Depot built in 1870, the museum focuses on the history of Grand Haven, Spring Lake and Ferrysburg.

HARBOR TROLLEY

☎ 616-842-3200; 440 North Ferry St; adult/child $1/50¢; ⏰ 11am-10pm Jun-Aug
These red trolleys double as historical tours of the area and public transportation. Most of all, they are good alternatives to fighting for a parking spot at the beach. The trolley leaves from Chinook Pier, travels to the state park and then heads to the heart of the city along Washington St to Bookman Municipal Park.

CHINOOK PIER

Grand Haven has one of the largest charter fishing fleets along Lake Michigan, with most of the boats docked at Chinook Pier off Jackson St. More than a dozen boats will take anglers several miles out onto Lake Michigan for an opportunity to land king salmon, lake trout and steelhead that occasionally exceed 20 pounds. The average rate for a half-day charter is $350-400 for one to four people. To book a trip, either head to the pier and talk to charter captains or get a complete list of them at the chamber of commerce. Even if you're not up to spending the morning holding a rod, the pier is interesting, particularly at the end of the day when the charters return and display their catch.

HOFFMASTER STATE PARK
☎ 231-798-3711; 6585 Lake Harbor Rd; vehicle $6

This 1100-acre park just north of Grand Haven offers some of the most interesting hiking in the area, with 10 miles of trails along steep, forested dunes and 2.5 miles of lakeshore. Before hitting the trail, stop at the park's **Gillette Sand Dune Visitor Center** (☎ 231-798-3573; 🕙 10am-4:30pm Tue-Sat, 12-4:30pm Sun June-Aug). The interpretive center provides an excellent overview of dune ecology and explains why Lake Michigan is home to so much sand.

SLEEPING

GRAND HAVEN STATE PARK
☎ 231-847-1309; 1001 Harbor Avenue; site $23

A mile from the downtown is this 48-acre urban park that draws huge crowds. Its main attraction is its wide beach. This is home to some of the finest sand along Lake Michigan and in the summer is a lively scene of sunbathers, windsurfers and swimmers. Despite being jammed together and little more than concrete pads, the 174 modern **campsites** (reservations ☎ 800-44-PARKS; www.michigan.gov/dnr) are almost always packed.

BLUE WATER INN
☎ 616-846-7431; www.bluewaterinngrandhaven.com; 1030 Harbor Dr; d $75-125

You won't find lodging any closer to the beach than this white inn. Its second-story deck is great for watching the sunset over Lake Michigan, while eight of its 14 rooms are more like small apartments with kitchenettes.

HARBOR HOUSE INN
☎ 616-846-0610, 800-841-0610; www.harborhousegh.com; 114 S Harbor Dr; d $150-250 includes breakfast

It's not quite historic, having been built in 1987, but the Harbor House does have a Victorian atmosphere with its long, wraparound porch, pink shutters and floral patterns on everything from the wallpaper to quilts. The 17 spacious rooms have private bathrooms and a few are equipped with whirlpool tubs.

FOUNTAIN INN

☎ 616-846-1800, 800-745-8660; www.fountain-inn-grandhaven.com; 1010 S Beacon Blvd (US 31); d $59-69 includes breakfast

The rooms are simple with no frills -- the reason, no doubt, that this is one of the best lodging deals in this high-price tourist town.

EATING

PONCHO'S

☎ 616-842-5555; 22 S Harbor Dr; mains $7-10; ⌚ 11:30am-10pm Mon-Thu, 11:30am-11pm Fri-Sun, 12-10pm Sun

This Mexican restaurant has a festive ambiance, outdoor seating overlooking the Grand River and a variety of enchiladas, burritos and tacos. Locals have voted its margaritas the best in town.

THE KIRBY GRILL

☎ 616-846-3299; 2 Washington St; mains $8-30; ⌚ 11:30am-11pm Mon-Thu, 11:30am-2am Fri-Sat, 11:30am-10pm Sun

The menu here ranges from soups and sandwiches to house special-ties such as grilled lamb chops and Parmesan-crusted chicken. This popular restaurant has outside seating on a second-floor patio with an excellent view of boat traffic on the river.

PAVILION'S WHARF DELI

☎ 616-842-9500; 18 Washington St; mains $4.50-6; ⌚ 7am-2:30pm Mon-Sat, 8am-1pm Sun

At this deli you can start out the day feasting on eggs in a jalapeño wrap and then, in the afternoon, switch to great hot subs or veggie sandwiches.

THE ROSEBUD OF GRAND HAVEN

☎ 616-846-7788; 100 Washington St; mains $5-17; ⌚ 11am-2am Mon-Sat, 5pm-2am Sun

This busy restaurant has fresh seafood, steaks, pizza and pasta. At night from Thursday to Saturday it's jamming with live music.

SHOPPING & ENTERTAINMENT

The heart of Grand Haven shopping is on Washington St, while nearby in Chinook Pier is the **farmers market** (☎ 616-842-4910; Jackson St; ⌚ 8am-2pm Wed & Sat Jun-Oct) where more than 30 farmers arrive with juicy local produce.

The climax of each summer night in Grand Haven is the **Musical Fountain** performance. The fountain occupies an area the size of a football field on the west side of the Grand River, and spectators watch the show from the **Waterfront Stadium** on the east side next to the museum. Synchronized to lights and music, 90,000 gallons of water spray into the air every night from Memorial to Labor Day and create a spectacular show.

The Coast Guard Festival (☎ 888-207-2434; www.ghcgfest.org) is celebrated the first week of August to honor the US Coast Guard. Events include waterfront entertainment, fireworks, a parade and a moving national memorial service for sailors lost at sea.

ON THE ROAD

Surrounding Muskegon Lake just 7 miles north of Grand Haven is the large urban area of **Muskegon** (pop 40,263), **Muskegon Heights** (pop 13,176) and **North Muskegon** (pop 2900), which you can easily bypass on US 31. To get a sense of how much money lumber barons made from Michigan white pine, visit the **Hackley & Hume National Historic Site** (☎ 231-722-0278; 484 W Webster Ave; adult/child $3/free; ☉ 12-4pm Wed-Sun May-Oct) in Muskegon. The site is made up of two mansions built side by side by Charles Hackley and his partner Thomas Hume. Construction reportedly required 200 craftsmen, millions of dollars and more than two years to complete.

If beaches and dunes are more to your liking, bypass Muskegon and exit US 31 at MI 120 on the north side of Muskegon Lake. Head west on MI 120 and then Memorial Dr and follow the signs to reach **Muskegon State Park** (☎ 231-744-3480; 3560 N Memorial Dr; vehicle $6, site $24). This 1165-acre park has 2 miles of sandy shoreline and 12 miles of trails in a backcountry of rugged dunes. Its Lake Michigan Campground is one of the oldest on the west side of the state and a favorite with tent campers.

Kids' Stuff

Children love Lake Michigan. What kid could possibly resist the best beaches and dunes in the Midwest? Here are attractions that will enthrall them:

- **Curious Kids Museum** (p10): Pilot the space shuttle at this children's museum in St Joseph.
- **Saugatuck Chain Ferry** (p15): Cross the Kalamazoo River on this quaint boat, then climb Mount Baldhead to reach Oval Beach.
- **Gillette Sand Dune Visitor Center** (p22): Learn about sand dunes in Hoffmaster State Park, and then climb the stairs to the Dune Overlook.
- **Tallship Manitou** (p41): Join a sailing adventure in Grand Traverse Bay on this schooner.
- **Dune Climb** (p33): Take a wild run down the state's most popular dune in Sleeping Bear Dunes National Lakeshore.
- **South Manitou Island** (p33): Board a ferry in Leland for this remote island to visit a lighthouse and snorkel around a shipwreck.
- **Fort Michilimackinac** (p55): Watch Redcoats fire muskets and cannons at this reconstructed 1715 fort.
- **Butterfly House** (p58): Step inside this center to see more than 400 butterflies fluttering about.

Within the park, Memorial Dr swings north and becomes Scenic Dr, a more interesting alternative to US 31 as it skirts Lake Michigan on the way to Whitehall. Within 7 miles you pass **Red Rooster Tavern** (☎ 231-744-4006; 2998 Scenic Dr; mains $5-14; 11:30am-12am Mon-Thu, 11:30am-2am Fri-Sat, 12pm-12am Sun), a good place to cool off and enjoy a cold beer on a hot summer day. More beaches and dunes – but no camping – are at **Duck Lake State Park** (☎ 231-744-3480; Scenic Dr; vehicle $6) a mile before Scenic Dr swings away from Lake Michigan and follows White Lake.

The twin towns of **Whitehall** (pop 3027) and **Montague** (pop 2276) are reached 12 miles from Muskegon State Park. These low-key towns are characterized by the **World's Largest Weathervane** erected by the Whitehall Metal Studios in 1984. The 48ft-high vane weighs 4300 pounds, has a 26ft-long arrow pointing north and is on Business US 31 on the north side of the White River in Montague. Right across the street is the southern end of the 22-mile **Hart-Montague Trail State Park**, Michigan's first rail trail and a popular bicycle route. For more information on the White Lake area, stop at the **White Lake Area Tourist Information Center** (☎ 231-893-4585; www.whitelake.org; 124 W Hanson St, Whitehall; 9am-5pm Mon-Fri, 9am-3pm Sat, 12-2pm Sun).

Another scenic alternative to US 31 is County Rd B15. The county road is the first exit north on Montague and curves its way into **Oceana County**, past many small township beaches on Lake Michigan and farm stands. Within 22 miles of departing US 31, you reach **Silver Lake**. The east side of the lake is jammed with motels, campgrounds, go-carts and miniature golf courses. The west side, between the inland lake and Lake Michigan is an 1800-acre tract of towering dunes.

These impressive dunes are part of **Silver Lake State Park** (☎ 231-873-3083; 9679 W State Park Rd; vehicle $6, site $23) and have been divided into three areas. A small section in the north is where you can drive your dune buggy, Jeep or other off-road vehicle. Not towing a dune buggy? You can rent a Jeep at **Sandy Korners Adventure Tours** (☎ 231-873-5048; www.sandykorners.com; 1762 N 24th Ave; $75-85 per hour; 9am-9pm Apr-Oct) and join a guided tour through the ORV area.

The south end of the dunes is where **Mac Wood's Dune Rides** (☎ 231-873-2817; www.macwoodsdunerides.com; 629 N 18th Ave; adult/child $13.50/9; 9:30am-dusk May-Oct) take place. Since 1930, the Wood family has been using large, open-air vehicles with balloon tires to take visitors on 40-minute tours up and down the dunes and along Lake Michigan.

The largest section is in the middle and designated for hikers who depart from a trailhead at the west end of Hazel Rd. It's a mile-long trudge across these windswept dunes to an isolated stretch of Lake Michigan. The mountains of sand are not an easy climb, but if you have the energy and a free afternoon, this is one of the most interesting treks in Michigan's dune country. Accommodations in Silver Lake include camping at the state park or **Sandy**

Shores Campground (☎ 231-873-3003; 8595 W Silver Lake Rd; sites $31-36) next door. There are also a variety of motels, the largest being **Silver Sands Resort** (☎ 231-873-3769; www.silversandsresort. net; 8446 W Hazel Rd; d $89-109), which has an assortment of rooms, 18 cottages and two private beaches on Silver Lake.

From Silver Lake County Rd, B15 continues north, passes a great beach at **Cedar Point County Park** and in 9 miles merges into Business US 31 at the east end of Pentwater Lake. You can take Business US 31 into **Pentwater**, an upscale resort area that surrounds a beautiful marina.

PENTWATER & LUDINGTON

Population: Pentwater 1050, Ludington 8500; Map 3

Only 14 miles from each other on US 31, Pentwater and Ludington are former sawmill towns that are worlds apart today as resort areas. Trendy Pentwater is an upscale community with restaurants and stores similar to Saugatuck. Much larger Ludington is a blue-collar town whose best-known gift shop is called Fort Daul and looks like a stockade. For information there's **Ludington Area Visitors Bureau** (☎ 877-420-6618;www.ludingtoncvb.com; 5300 W US 10; ⏱ 8am-5pm Mon-Fri) or **Pentwater Chamber of Commerce** (☎ 866-869-4150; www.pentwater.org; 324 S Hancock St; ⏱ 10am-3:30pm Mon-Fri, 9:30am-12pm Sat).

SIGHTS & ACTIVITIES

CHARLES MEARS STATE PARK
☎ 231-869-2051; Lowell St, Pentwater; vehicle $6, site $23

This 50-acre park has the best beach in Pentwater. Overlooking the beach is a campground with 179 modern **sites** (☎ 800-47-PARKS; www.michigan.gov/dnr) filled almost daily from mid-June through August. From 11am-4pm daily in the summer the **Air-Fun Kite Shop** (☎ 231-869-7004; 167 S Hancock St) has kites and somebody on the beach giving free flying lessons.

LUDINGTON STATE PARK
☎ 231-842-8671; M-116, Ludington; vehicle $6, site $23

At the foot of US 10 in Ludington is Stearns Park with a beach that is at least 50 yards wide. But for a beach of your own, head north on MI 116 to **Ludington State Park**, a 5,300-acre gem with 5 miles of sandy Lake Michigan shoreline and more beach on Hamlin Lake. On the way to the park, people simply pull over on MI 116 and head for the surf. Once in the park you can hike 1.5 miles out to **Big Sable Point Lighthouse** (☎ 231-845-7343; www.bigsablelighthouse.org; adult/child $2/1; ⏱ 10am-6pm) that was built in 1867 and today is a museum. Ludington also has 344 **sites** (☎ 800-47-PARKS; www.michigan.gov/dnr) that are as popular as those in Mears State Park.

HISTORIC WHITE PINE VILLAGE

☎ 231-843-4808; www.historicwhitepinevillage.com; 1687 S Lakeshore Dr, Ludington; adult/child $6/4; ⏱ 10am-5pm Tue-Sat

This museum complex overlooks Lake Michigan and features 25 historic buildings ranging from a trapper's cabin and a doctor's office to an old-fashioned ice cream parlor. Staffed by costumed guides, White Pine is like strolling through a small town in the late 1800s.

SLEEPING & EATING

NICKERSON INN

☎ 800-742-1288; www.nickersoninn.com; 262 W Lowell St, Pentwater; d $150-250 includes breakfast

This historic inn is near Mears State Park and has been serving beachgoers since 1914. The inn has 13 rooms, including suites with Jacuzzis, and a dining room where, in the evening, you can watch the sun melt into Lake Michigan.

HEXAGON HOUSE

☎ 231-869-4102; www.hexagonhouse.com; 760 Sixth St, Pentwater; d $150-200

Built in 1896, the Hexagon House is Pentwater's most unusual B&B, featuring long, wraparound porches on two floors. It has five rooms in Victorian decor and is within easy walking distance of the downtown area.

PARKVIEW COTTAGES

☎ 231-843-4445; 803 W Fitch St, Ludington; cottage $108-125

Ludington has far more affordable lodging than Pentwater, including Parkview Cottages, just a block from Stearns Park. The 11 cottages sleep four to six easily and surround a large outdoor deck with a gas grill.

VIKING ARMS INN

☎ 231-843-3441; 903 E Ludington Ave, Ludington; d $70-110

A mile from Stearns Park, this motel has large, clean rooms and an outdoor heated pool.

THE VILLAGE PUB & CAFÉ

☎ 231-869-4626; 347 S Hancock St; mains $17-23; ⏱ 11:30am-9pm

This restaurant offers a full menu, including the customary whitefish and lake perch. Outside, a pleasant deck overlooks the marina.

JAMESPORT BREWING CO

☎ 231-845-2522; 410 S James St; mains $10-19; ⏱ 11:30am-10pm Sun-Thu, 11:30am-10:30pm Fri-Sat

Ludington's best restaurant is this brewpub, which opened in 2000 in an old brick warehouse. Enjoy a wide-ranging menu that includes shepherds pie, Thai peanut noodles and veggie burgers. Wash it down with a pint of locally crafted beer.

SHOPPING & ENTERTAINMENT

Pentwater's most unusual business is **Brass Anchor Ships Store** (☎ 231-869-4200; 500 S Hancock St), which sells marine supplies in the back of the shop and displays nautical antiques and art in the front. In Ludington, **Fort Daul** (☎ 231-843-2890; 101 W Ludington St; ✪ 11am-8pm) is two floors packed with every touristy souvenir ever made in China and Taiwan. Kids love this place more than the beach.

There are free weekly concerts from July through August in both Ludington (✪ 7pm Wed at Waterfront Park) and Pentwater (✪ 8pm Thu at Village Green). If it's Sunday, head to **Gull Landing Restaurant** (☎ 231-869-4215; 438 S Hancock St, Pentwater; ✪ 7am-11pm), which turns its large outdoor deck over to a jazz band.

ON THE ROAD

It's a 28-mile drive via US 10 and US 31 from Ludington to Manistee, and along the way you skirt the wildest stretch of Lake Michigan. Here **Ludington State Park** merges into **Nordhouse Dunes Wilderness** to create a 9,000-acre tract with almost 10 miles of undeveloped shoreline. The best way to explore this area is to pitch a tent at the **Lake Michigan Recreation Area** (☎ 231-723-2211; Lake Michigan Rd; site $13), 8 miles east of US 31. The campground is rustic but overlooks a beautiful beach and has a trail system that leads into the wilderness.

MANISTEE

Population 6700; Map 7

In 1890 Manistee boasted seven millionaire lumber barons as residents and a good number more worth half that much. All that money and timber resulted in a port city filled with history, Victorian mansions and a grand stage theater. Add great beaches and nearby wilderness, and you have one of the most interesting

---

LAKE MICHIGAN CAR FERRY

The **SS Badger** (☎ 888-227-7447; www.ssbadger.com; 701 Maritime Dr, Ludington; roundtrip fare adult/child $78/36) is the last of the great car ferries that hit their peaks in the 1950s, when almost a dozen vessels transported more than 200,000 people and 71,000 cars across Lake Michigan annually. The ferry departs Ludington at 8am and 7:55pm for Manitowoc, Wisconsin, daily during the summer. For a great day trip, take a bike ($5 each way) on the 8am sailing and spend the day riding the paved Mariners Trail to Rawley Point Lighthouse, a roundtrip of 25 miles, before returning to Ludington on the 12:30am run.

towns along Lake Michigan. For more information, contact the **Manistee Visitors Center** (☎ 877-626-4783; www.visitmanistee.com; 310 First St; ⏱ 9am-7pm Mon-Wed, 9am-8pm Thu-Fri, 10am-4pm Sat, 10am-2pm Sun).

SIGHTS & ACTIVITIES

MUSEUMS
Manistee has several historical buildings that have been turned into small museums. The most interesting is the **Manistee County Historical Museum** (☎ 231-723-5531; 425 River St; adult/family $2/5; ⏱ 10am-5pm Mon-Sat), housed in the old Lyman Drugstore which dates back to 1903. The **Manistee Fire Hall** (☎ 231-723-1549; 281 1st St; admission free; ⏱ 8am-5pm) was built in 1888 and is the oldest continuous operating station in Michigan. It's a classic Romanesque Revival brick building with a small area of historical displays inside.

HISTORICAL TOURS
You can pick up a *Historical Walking Tour* brochure at the visitors center or hop on the **Manistee Trolley** (☎ 231-723-6561; 180 Memorial Dr; $3; ⏱ 11am, 12pm & 1pm Jun-Sep) for an hour-long narrated tour of the downtown area.

SS CITY OF MILWAUKEE
☎ 231-398-0328; www.carferry.com; 111 Arthur St (US 31); adult/child $6/4; ⏱ 12-5pm Wed-Sun Jun-Aug
This 350ft vessel was launched in 1930 and was the last of the great railroad ferries that carried entire freight trains across Lake Michigan. Today a national historic landmark, the *City of Milwaukee* is being restored and is open for hourlong tours that take you everywhere onboard, from the giant engines to the men's smoking room.

RIVERWALK
The shoreline of the Manistee River downtown has been turned into a 1.5-mile walkway lined with historical displays. Anchored right off the walkway are charter fishing captains and **Water Bug Boat Tours** (☎ 231-398-0919, River St; adult/child $10/5; ⏱ 1pm & 3pm Jun-Aug), which offers hourlong tours up the river.

BEACHES
There are several beaches in and around the city. The most popular one is **1st St Beach** at Douglas Park on the corner of 1st and Cherry Sts. This is another wide, sandy beach. Douglas Park has picnic facilities, playscapes, basketball and volleyball courts, and is the start of the Riverwalk.

SLEEPING & EATING

Manistee doesn't have great dining. The best restaurant in the area is 6 miles north in Onekama, the **Blue Slipper Bistro** (☎ 231-889-4045;

8058 First St; mains $13-19; 🕙 11am-9:30pm Sun-Thu, 11am-10pm Fri-Sat), known for fresh pasta and seafood. In the morning, locals crowd **Goody's Juice & Java** (☎ 231-398-9580; 343 River St; sandwiches $4-6; 🕙 7am-8pm Mon-Sat, 8am-3pm Sun) for espresso drinks, smoothies and baked goods.

RAMSDELL INN
☎ 888-823-8310, 231-398-7901; www.ramsdellinn.net; 399 River St; d $99-189

This boutique hotel offers eight rooms and two suites right in the heart of downtown Manistee. The building, built in 1891 as a bank and restored in 2003, is classic Victorian with hand-carved woodwork and stained-glass windows.

LAKESHORE MOTEL
☎ 231-723-2667; 101 S Lakeshore Dr; d $78-90

The 21 rooms in this motel are plain and simple, but the location is hard to beat, right across from 1st St Beach. You hit sand the minute you step out the door.

ORCHARD BEACH STATE PARK
☎ 231-723-7422; MI 115 (Lakeshore Dr); site $20

This 201-acre state park has 168 sites on a bluff above a Lake Michigan beach. Orchard Beach is not nearly as popular Ludington State Park, but it would be wise to **reserve** (☎ 800-47-PARKS; www.michigan.gov/dnr) sites on the weekends.

ENTERTAINMENT

The impressive **Ramsdell Theatre** (☎ 231-723-7188; 101 Maple St; tickets $15-20) was built in 1903 and is where James Earl Jones began his stage career. Today it is home to the Manistee Civic Players, who offer productions year-round. **Little River Resort** (☎ 866-466-7338; www.littlerivercasino.com; US 31 & M-22; 🕙 24hr) is a tribal casino just north of town with 1200 slot machines, table games and several restaurants.

ON THE ROAD

It's hard to imagine a more interesting route along the Lake, or anywhere in Michigan for that matter, than MI 22. The state highway begins near Manistee and hugs the shoreline for 115 miles, first along Lake Michigan and then south along Grand Traverse Bay to Traverse City. It also skirts the famous Sleeping Bear Dunes and passes so many inland lakes, quaint towns and historic lighthouses that *National Geographic* magazine once called it 'Michigan's most scenic drive.'

Within 5 miles of Manistee, MI 22 reaches Portage Lake and the small town of **Onekama**. Nearby is the **Portage Point Inn** (☎ 800-878-7248; www.portagepointinn.com; 8513 S Portage Point Dr;

d $159-189/849-999 day/week). The resort opened in 1903 during the steamship era as a summer retreat for wealthy Chicago families and among its guests were (reputedly) Al Capone and later Orson Welles. Today this historic and lavish inn offers hotel rooms, cottages and condos along with two beaches, one on Portage Lake, the other on Lake Michigan.

Ten miles from Onekama, MI 22 swings around Arcadia Lake and then follows the high bluffs that line Lake Michigan to the north. Here you pass several scenic turnouts, with the best, **Inspiration Point**, reached 1.5 miles north of the town of **Arcadia**. At 1300ft this is the highest point along Lake Michigan, and the picnic area includes a massive observation deck with a view that is endless on a clear day. In another 10 miles (or 33 miles from Manistee) you arrive at the twin towns of **Elberta** (pop 478) and the much larger **Frankfort** (pop 1546), surrounding Betsie Lake. Both towns maintain a municipal beach on Lake Michigan. Tired of whitefish? **The Fusion** (☎ 231-352-4114; 411 Main St; mains $6-11; ☼ 8am-9pm

---

DETOUR: BENZIE COUNTY

Not every attraction in Benzie County is wedged between Crystal Lake and Lake Michigan along MI 22. In Elberta, you can head east on River Rd to reach tiny **Benzonia**. Along the way stop at **Gwen Frostic Presscraft Papers** (☎ 231-882-5505; 5140 River Rd; ☼ 9am-4:30pm) to watch 15 classic Heidelberg presses clanking out notepaper, cards, books and placemats using the original blocks carved by the late artist, one of Northern Michigan's best loved. More handcrafted treats are 5 miles east of Benzonia via Traverse Rd, which turns into Homestead Rd. Located in a quirky farmhouse in seemingly the middle of nowhere is the **Homestead Sugar House** (☎ 231-882-7712; 11393 Homestead Rd; ☼ 9:30am-5pm Wed-Mon), Benzie County's oldest candy-making shop. Enjoy the aroma of hand-dipped cherries, fresh toffee and mouthwatering maple creams while the owner, dressed Grandma Moses-style, entices you with samples.

There are two excellent restaurants in Benzonia and nearby Beulah. Northern Michigan's best margaritas are at the **Roadhouse Mexican Bar & Grill** (☎ 231-882-9631; 1058 US 31; mains $10-16; ☼ 11am-10pm Sun-Mon, 11am-11pm Fri-Sat). Further north on US 31 is the **Cherry Hut** (☎ 231-882-4431; 216 US 31; mains $10-16; ☼ 10am-10pm) with its trademark bright red smiling pie sign. The Cherry Hut is renowned for its cherry pies and you can either buy one to go or enjoy a slice ($2.75) in this always-bustling restaurant.

To relive the 1950s, continue north on US 31 for 4 miles to the **Cherry Bowl Drive-In** (☎ 231-325-3413; 9812 Honor Hwy; adult/child $7.50/free). Northern Michigan's last drive-in theater has been showing movies since 1953 and still honors that swinging era by serving malts and chili fries in its diner while workers dress as if they were the cast of *Happy Days*. Admission includes two movies, and kids 12 and younger are free. Families haven't paid so little to see a movie since, well, the 1950s.

Mon-Thu, 8am-10pm Fri-Sat, 8am-8pm Sun) in Frankfort features a menu of Eastern and Western cuisine, ranging from Thai tofu salad and almond chicken to eggs sunny-side up for breakfast. The **Hotel Frankfort** (☎ 231-352-4303; www.brooksideinn.com; 231 Main St; d $185-270, includes breakfast and dinner) is famous as a romantic getaway complete with mirrored canopy beds and in-room Polynesian spas. For the less passionate, there is **Harbor Lights** (☎ 231-352-9614, 800-346-9614; www.harborlightsmotel.com; 15 Second St; d $130-145) with rooms and suites overlooking the Frankfort North Breakwater Lighthouse.

To the north, MI 22 skirts Crystal Lake and in 6 miles from Frankfort reaches **Point Betsie Lighthouse** (www.pointbetsie.org; Point Betsie Rd; $2; ☟ 10am-5pm Thu-Sun Jun-Aug). Built in 1858, this is one of the most picturesque and probably the most photographed of Michigan's 116 lighthouses. Overlooking Crystal Lake nearby is **Chimney Corners Resort** (☎ 231-352-7522; www.chimneycornersresort.com; 1602 Crystal Dr; cottages per week $1075-1825, d $75 shared bathroom). This woodsy resort has a variety of rooms and log cottages, a beach on the lake and a dining hall with a rustic Northern Michigan decor.

One and one-half miles from Chimney Corners, MI 22 enters the Sleeping Bear Dunes National Lakeshore and passes the trailhead for **Old Indian Trail**. It's a mile hike along this trail to a relatively isolated and beautiful stretch of Lake Michigan beach.

SLEEPING BEAR DUNES NATIONAL LAKESHORE

Map 9

Lake Michigan is home to the world's largest collection of freshwater dunes, and its crowning jewel is Sleeping Bear Dunes National Lakeshore, the only national park in the Lower Peninsula. Established in 1970, the 74,000-acre park stretches from Frankfort almost to Leland and includes 30 miles of shoreline, some of the largest dunes in Michigan and two remote islands in Lake Michigan. It also offers the best day hiking south of the Mackinac Bridge.

Plan at least a full day in the park, two or three if you want to include a few hikes. The first stop should be the park's **Philip Hart Visitor Center** (☎ 231-326-5134; www.nps.gov/slbe; 9922 Front St; ☟ 8am-9pm) in Empire to purchase a vehicle park pass (week/annual $10/20). Also inside are exhibits, a video theater, trail maps and a bookstore.

SIGHTS & ACTIVITIES

PIERCE STOCKING SCENIC DRIVE

The park's most stunning scenery is viewed from this 7.5-mile one-way loop maintained by the National Park Service, located 2 miles north of the visitor center on MI 109. The speed limit is only 15mph, but even that seems too fast, as you are constantly stopping to enjoy lofty views from observation areas. The route includes a bike lane, but the hilly dunes make this ride quite a workout.

THE DUNE CLIMB

The most famous dune in Michigan is the Dune Climb, 4 miles north of the visitor center on MI 109. Every year more than 320,000 visitors trudge up this steep, open dune for a wild and sandy run back down.

At the top are exceptional views of Glen Lake and the start of the **Dunes Trail** (see Hiking, below), at the bottom a picnic area.

GLEN HAVEN HISTORIC DISTRICT

☎ 231-334-3710; MI 109; vehicle pass; ☽ 11am-4pm Jul-Sep

What was lumber baron DH Day's company town in the mid-1800s is now the Glen Haven Historic District, with several of the buildings restored as museums. You can view a collection of historic wooden boats at the **Cannery Boathouse**, watch horseshoes made at the **Blacksmith Shop** or step inside a 1920s general store.

SLEEPING BEAR POINT MARITIME MUSEUM

No Phone; MI 209; vehicle pass; ☽ 10:30am-5pm May-Sep

A half-mile west of Glen Haven is Sleeping Bear Point Maritime Museum, a former US Lifesaving Station and boathouse filled with maritime exhibits. Highlights of the museum are the daily reenactments rangers stage of 19th-century rescue techniques.

HIKING

Thanks to the high vistas and open country created by the dunes, Sleeping Bear Dunes offers spectacular day hiking. The park maintains a dozen trails on the mainland and more on South and North Manitou Islands (see **The Islands**, below). One of the most popular is the **Dunes Trail**, a 4.5-mile roundtrip trek from the top of the Dune Climb to a remote stretch of Lake Michigan shoreline. Northeast of Glen Arbor at the end of Port Oneida Rd is the **Pyramid Point Trail**, which includes Pyramid Point, an 840ft-high lakeshore dune that once was a popular launch site for hang gliders. More edge-of-the-bluff views are found along **Empire Bluff Trail**, a 2-mile walk from Wilco Rd in Empire. **Platte Plains Trail** (M-22, 9.5 miles south of Empire) is a 15-mile network of paths that includes a backcountry camping area and beautiful beaches.

THE ISLANDS

Sleeping Bear Dunes also includes a pair of islands that are reached by ferry service from Leland. **Manitou Island Transit** (☎ 231-256-9061; www.leelanau.com/manitou) makes daily runs to 5360-acre **South Manitou Island** and the 15,000-acre **North Manitou Island** for a roundtrip fare of adult/child $25/14 to either. There are no stores or facilities other than campgrounds on the islands, but at South Manitou the ferry lays over for four hours, making a day trip possible. The island includes a lighthouse, three campgrounds, some great beaches and two shipwrecks; one can be viewed by snorkeling. The much larger North Manitou is a backpacker's haven, with most people spending three days to hike its 17-mile perimeter.

SLEEPING

Sleeping Bear Dunes has two campgrounds for car campers and RVers, plus walk-in campgrounds at Platte Plains Trail and both islands. Back-country camping is also allowed on North Manitou Island.

PLATTE RIVER CAMPGROUND
☎ 231-325-5881; M-22; walk-in/rustic/electricity $12/16/21

Located 12 miles south of Empire, this NPS campground has 174 sites, including 25 delightful walk-in sites. Near the campground are trailheads for **Platte Plains Trail** (p33) and one of the most beautiful beaches in Michigan, where the Platte River empties into Lake Michigan. This **campground** (☎ 800-365-2267; http://reservations.nps.gov) is a favorite, so reserve a site in advance.

DH DAY CAMPGROUND
☎ 231-326-5134; M-109; site $12

Just east of Glen Arbor is DH Day, with 88 rustic sites. It lacks the hookups and modern restrooms of Platte River, but a short walk away is another great Lake Michigan beach. DH Day is also very popular, but sites are handed out first-come, first-serve. Get there early in the morning!

GLEN ARBOR & LELAND

Map 9

From Glen Haven, MI 109 swings east and rejoins MI 22 in Glen Arbor, a small village that bustles in the summer with shops, restaurants and galleries. Beyond Glen Arbor, MI 22 reenters the Sleeping Bear National Lakeshore briefly and in 8 miles returns to the edge of Lake Michigan, hugging the shoreline all the way to Leland. The best place for information on the area is the **Leelanau Peninsula Chamber of Commerce** (☎ 800-980-9895; www.leelanau-chamber.com; 5046 SW Bayshore Dr, Suttons Bay; 🕙 10am-4pm Mon-Sat).

SIGHTS & ACTIVITIES

SHIPWRECKS

The beaches west of Glen Arbor are a trail past shipwrecks in the Manitou Passage. Between 1850 and 1900 more than 50 vessels sank in this narrow, shoal-lined channel between the Manitou Islands and the mainland, the vast majority within 400 yards of the beach. Often you can find pieces of the boats washed ashore, particularly after storms. Pick up the brochure *Beachcombing for Shipwrecks* at DH Day

Campground, on MI 109 2 miles west of Glen Arbor, to learn what you're looking for and how to age the pieces you find.

LEELANAU HISTORICAL MUSEUM
☎ 231-256-7475; www.leelanauhistory.org; 203 E Cedar St; adult/child $2/1; ☼ 10am-4pm Tue-Sat
This interesting museum covers the cultural history of the peninsula and the surrounding islands, beginning with the first people to inhabit the area, the Anishnabek. Maritime artifacts and an antique toy collection are also part of the permanent gallery.

MANITOU ISLAND TRANSIT
☎ 231-256-9061; www.leelanau.com/manitou; 207 W River St, Leland; adult/child $15/10; ☼ departs 6:30pm Mon, Wed, Fri-Sat
The company that takes you to the Manitou Islands also has a sunset cruise along the Sleeping Bear Dunes National Lakeshore. The ferry departs from Leland and passes such landmarks as Good Harbor Bay, Pyramid Point and the North Manitou Shoal Lighthouse, finishing the trip with the sun dipping below the watery horizon of Lake Michigan.

CRYSTAL RIVER CANOE LIVERY
☎ 231-334-3090; 6052 W River Rd; Glen Arbor; canoe/kayak $25/$15-20
The Crystal River is one of the clearest rivers in the Lower Peninsula, and because much of it flows through state land, it is not lined with a cottage on every bend. It's an easy 7-mile, 2.5-hour paddle from its headwaters on Fish Lake back to this livery, which operates at a Shell Station on MI 22.

SLEEPING

GLEN ARBOR B&B
☎ 231-334-6789, 877-253-4200; www.glenarborbnb.com; 6548 Western Ave, Glen Arbor; d $105-165 includes breakfast; May-Nov
Situated in the heart of Glen Arbor, this century-old farmhouse has been renovated as a French country inn with six themed rooms.

THE INN
☎ 231-334-5100; www.thehomesteadresort.com; 1 Ridge Rd, Glen Arbor; d $173-356, suites $235-566
Part of the Homestead, a golf and ski resort, this luxurious inn has a beautiful location overlooking the mouth of the Crystal River on Lake Michigan. At the resort you can choose between the pool or the beach, or explore dune country on Bay View Trail, part of the national lakeshore trail system.

SNOWBIRD INN
☎ 231-256-9773; www.snowbirdinn.com; 473 Manitou Tr, Leland; d $125-150 includes breakfast
Surrounded by 18 acres of cherry orchards and gardens is this quaint

farmhouse with a large, rambling porch. The turn-of-the-century decor is tasteful but not overwhelming.

LELAND LODGE

☎ 231-256-9848; www.lelandlodge.com; 565 Pearl St, Leland; d $99-189

This resort includes a main hotel and six cottages overlooking the Leland Golf Course. Enjoy a drink on the outdoor deck while watching duffers play through, or head inside to the dining room for a fine meal with a bottle of local wine. The comfortable rooms have a woodsy ambiance.

EATING

THE GOOD HARBOR GRILL

☎ 231-334-3555; 6584 Western Ave, Glen Arbor; mains $7-18; 🕑 5:30am-9:30pm

A bright-blue restaurant with a sailboat theme, the Good Harbor Grill serves a variety of dishes, including vegetarian entrees, soups and sandwiches.

THE WESTERN AVENUE GRILL

☎ 231-334-3362; 6410 Western Ave, Glen Arbor; mains $8-19; 🕑 11am-10pm Sun-Thu, 11am-11pm Fri-Sat

Looking like a giant log cabin and doubling as a sports bar at night, this restaurant specializes in fresh fish (who doesn't in Northern Michigan?) but also serves homemade pastas, pizza, steaks and sandwiches.

THE BLUEBIRD

☎ 231-256-9081; 102 E River St, Leland; mains $14-18; 🕑 5-10pm

Leland's best-known restaurant overlooks the Leland River and features seafood, steaks and locally caught fish alongside an extensive wine list. Instead of bread before the main course, waiters bring out baskets of warm cinnamon rolls.

THE COVE

☎ 231-256-9834; 111 W River St, Leland; mains $8-20; 🕑 11am-10pm May-Oct

Haven't had your whitefish yet? The Cove prepares the Great Lakes specialty four different ways and serves it with a cup of seafood chowder full of shrimp, crab and clams, all at a table overlooking Fishtown.

SHOPPING & ENTERTAINMENT

Glen Arbor is punctuated with art galleries and gift shops. Be sure to stop by the world's largest cherry retailer, the **Cherry Republic** (☎ 231-334-3150, 800-206-6949; www.cherryrepublic.com; 6026 S Lake St; 🕑 8am-10:30pm), where everything is literally cherry. Shop for dried cherries, cherry salsa or salad bowls carved out of cherry wood. Or step into the café for 12 different flavors of cherry ice cream or a cherry hot dog.

In Leland, most shoppers head to **Fishtown**, a collection of gray and weather-beaten shacks on the water. What were ice- and

Searching for Petoskey Stones

A popular activity in Northern Michigan and an obsession with some tourists is hunting for Petoskey stones, Michigan's state stone, which feature a distinct honeycomb pattern.

The stones are actually petrified coral, leftover fragments of the reefs that existed 350 million years ago when warm-water seas covered the northern half of the state. There are Petoskey stones lying on beaches from Frankfort to Alpena, and the best time to search for them is after foul weather, when a strong westerly wind kicks up the surf and rolls a whole new set above the breakline.

Get there early! Rock hounds will descend on the newly exposed gems like seagulls on a hot-dog bun. Then walk along the shore in 1 to 2ft of water, constantly picking up handfuls of pebbles and holding them just under the clear surface of the lake. Dry Petoskey stones are silvery with no apparent markings to the untrained eye, but when the stones are wet it's easy to see the telltale rings of the coral.

Some good beaches to search are **Platte Bay** in Sleeping Bear Dunes National Lakeshore, **Peterson Park** west of Northport off of Peterson Park Rd, **Fisherman's Island State Park** south of Charlevoix and, of course, **Petoskey State Park** near Harbor Springs.

smoke-houses serving commercial fisherman a century ago are now a collection of art, gift and clothing shops, many with maritime themes. **Carlson's Fisheries** (☎ 231-256-9801; 205 W River Rd; 8am-8pm May-Sep) still unloads its catch here and sells delicious smoked whitefish and homemade fish sausage.

Both towns have bars for some late-night fun. **Arts Tavern** (☎ 231-334-3754; 6487 Western Ave; 7am-2:30am) in Glen Arbor is a popular hangout with a nice selection of beer on tap and pool tables. Between Leland and Northport is the lively **Happy Hour Bar** (☎ 231-386-9923; 7100 N Manitou Tr; 11am-11:30pm), which serves one of the best hamburgers on the Leelanau Peninsula.

NORTHPORT & SUTTONS BAY

Population 1200; Map 4

Suttons Bay and Northport are button-cute and good destinations for an easy day trip if you're staying in Traverse City (p40). Suttons Bay is only 15 miles from the Cherry Capital via MI 22. Northport is another 11 miles north of Suttons Bay and is where MI 22 swings south to begin skirting Lake Michigan.

SIGHTS & ACTIVITIES

BEACHES

Both Northport and Suttons Bay have public beaches on the calmer and usually warmer Grand Traverse Bay. A great walk-in beach is on **Cathead Bay** in Leelanau State Park and is reached from Northport by heading north on MI 201 and CR 629 for four miles and then west on Densmore Rd. The shortest route to Lake Michigan is the half-mile **Lake Michigan Trail**.

INLAND SEAS EDUCATION ASSOCIATION

☎ 231-271-3077; www.greatlakeseducation.org; 100 Pame St, Suttons Bay; $30-65

This nonprofit education group uses a tallship schooner as a classroom for a variety of environmental programs while cruising Grand Traverse Bay and Lake Michigan. Trips include Power Island for a day hike and an astronomy cruise, in which the ships leave at sunset and return at night.

VINEYARDS

A highlight of this region is a visit to one of the dozen wineries spread across the peninsula. All have tasting rooms and sell wine on site, either by bottles or by the case. Overlooking Lake Leelanau, **Boskydel Vineyards** (☎ 231-256-7272; 2881 S Lake Leelanau Dr; 1-6pm) is one of the oldest and most scenic vineyards and offers very affordable whites. Madonna may not live in Michigan anymore, but her father does, and he produces Pinot Grigio and Chardonnay at his **Ciccone Vineyard & Winery** (☎ 231-271-5552; www.cicconevineyards. com; 10343 E Hilltop Rd; 12-6pm). The best sparkling wine can be found at **L Mawby Vineyards** (☎ 231-271-3522; www.lmawby.com; 4519 S Elm Rd; 12-6pm).

LEELANAU TRAIL

This 15-mile rail trail extends from Carter Rd on the west side of Traverse City to Suttons Bay and by 2006 will be connected to the TART trail (p40). Six miles are paved at the southern end and the rest is a two track, best suited for mountain bikers and hikers.

GRAND TRAVERSE LIGHTHOUSE MUSEUM

☎ 231-386-7195; www.grandtraverselighthouse.com; 15500 North Lighthouse Point Rd; adult/child $2/1; 10am-7pm May-Oct

At the tip of the peninsula in Leelanau State Park is the Grand Traverse Lighthouse, which has guided sailors around the tip of the peninsula since 1858. Today, you can tour the restored lightkeeper's home, read exhibits about foghorns and shipwrecks and then climb the tower for a view of Lake Michigan

SLEEPING

LEELANAU STATE PARK

☎ 231-386-5422; 15310 N Lighthouse Point Rd, Northport; sites $10

Most of this 1350-acre park is a separate area around Cathead Bay with only hiking trails. The campground, however, is at the tip of the peninsula and offers 52 rustic sites with 10 of them right on the bay. Despite being rustic, this is a very popular campground. Call for **reservations** (☎ 800-44-PARKS; www.michigan.gov/dnr).

SUNRISE LANDING MOTEL & RESORT
☎ 231-386-5010, 800-488-5762; www.sunriselanding.com; 6530 W Bayshore Dr, Northport; d $94-134

Three miles south of Northport, this motel has its own beach and themed rooms, some with kitchenettes, whirlpools and fireplaces.

RED LION MOTOR LODGE
☎ 231-271-6694, 877-567-7639; www.redlionmotorlodge.com; 4290 W Bay Shore Dr, Suttons Bay; d $115-125

On the more economical end of peninsula lodging, if $115 a night can be called economical, is this motel. Its rooms are not lavish, but they are clean.

THE VINEYARD INN ON SUTTONS BAY
☎ 231-941-7060; www.vininn.com; 1338 N Pebble Beach, Suttons Bay; suites $195-250

This historic inn has been renovated with a stylish European-country theme that creates a nice ambiance mixing the old and the new. All suites have lake views.

EATING

THE WILLOWBROOK
☎ 231-386-5617; 201 Mill St, Northport; mains $4-5.50; ⏰ 7am-8pm Mon-Sat, 7am-3pm Sun

On a babbling brook (thus the name), this restaurant doubles as a antique shop and ice cream parlor but also serves affordable breakfast and lunches.

EAT'S SPOT
☎ 231-386-7536; 215 Mill St, Northport; mains $4.50-9; ⏰ 11am-9pm Mon-Thu, 11am-9pm Fri

This small restaurant downtown is known for its soups, but it also serves pizza, sandwiches, salads and espresso drinks.

CAFÉ BLISS
☎ 231-271-500; 420 St Josephs Ave, Suttons Bay; mains $16-30; ⏰ 5pm-10pm

In a charming, green building, this café has garden dining and an interesting menu featuring ethnic and vegetarian dishes and a nice wine list. Reservations are recommended.

HATTIES
☎ 231-271-6222; 111 St Joseph Ave, Suttons Bay; mains $26-29; ⏰ 5:30-9:30pm

This award-winning restaurant serves an innovative cuisine inspired by regional ingredients such as morel mushrooms, whitefish and other local produce. Hatties is truly an exceptional dining experience, often featuring dishes such as morel ravioli and wild salmon with cilantro and lime.

ENTERTAINMENT

The fourth Saturday of July is the **Suttons Bay Jazz Festival**, a day of food, Leelanau wine and lots of jazz. Purchase **tickets** (☎ 231-271-4444; $20-30) in advance if possible, as this event is well attended. The **Leelanau Sands Casino** (☎ 231-271-4104; 2521 West Bay Dr; ☺ 10am-2pm) near Suttons Bay is owned by the same Native American tribe that runs Turtle Creek Casino in Traverse City. Along with slot machines and table games, the resort has restaurants and entertainment.

TRAVERSE CITY

Population 15,155; Map 10

There is much more to Michigan's Cherry Capital than the plump, red fruit. Overlooking the Grand Traverse Bay, Traverse City is the largest city in Northern Michigan and has the reputation of being clean, safe, and most importantly, a fun place. The city's main event is the National Cherry Festival, held in the first week of July, a time when tourists arrive in droves and locals leave. The very helpful **Traverse City Convention and Visitors Bureau** (☎ 231-947-1120, 800-940-1120; www.mytraversecity.com; 101 W Grandview Ave; 9am-6pm Mon-Fri) has racks of brochures on the area.

SIGHTS & ACTIVITIES

CLINCH PARK & ZOO
☎ 231-922-4904; 400 Boardman Ave; adult/child $3/1.50; ☺ 9:30am-5:30pm Apr-Nov

You don't have to go tramping through the woods to encounter wildlife. This park in the heart of downtown includes a zoo filled with animals native to Michigan – wolves, elk and bears, among others. The most popular attraction in the zoo, however, is the red minitrain that loops around it. The park is also home to Traverse City's nicest beach.

TART TRAIL

This paved rail trail begins at M-72 in Acme and extends 11 miles to the west side of the city, allowing cyclists, in-line skaters and walkers to reach the downtown area, three lovely beaches, and the Clinch Zoo while avoiding the rush hour–like traffic.

Several bike shops have bicycle rentals for around $20 a day. **McLain Cycle & Fitness** (☎ 231-941-7161; www.mclaincycle.com; 750 E 8th St; ☺ 10am-6pm Mon-Fri, 9am-5pm Sat, 11am-4pm Sun) is located right on the TART Trail. **Brick Wheels** (☎ 231-947-4274; 736 E 8th St; ☺ 9am-6pm Mon-Thu, 9am-8pm Fri, 9am-4pm Sat, 11am-3pm Sun) also rents in-line skates and is next door.

SAILING

Boating is very popular on beautiful Grand Traverse Bay, and Traverse City doesn't lack companies willing to take you on a cruise. **The Nauticat** (☎ 231-947-1730; www.nauti-cat.com; in front of Holiday Inn on West Bay St; $15-35) is a 47ft catamaran that has several tours a day, including the Kid Cruise, in which children can help with the sails, and the Champagne Sunset Cruise. If catamarans aren't your sailing style, maybe a replica of a 19th-century schooner with white magnificent sails is. The **Manitou** (☎ 231-941-2000, 800-678-0383; www.tallshipsailing.com; 13390 W Bay Shore Dr; adult/child $32-39/16-24) sails three times a day and features live music onboard Tuesday nights.

GRAND TRAVERSE BALLOONS

☎ 231-947-7433; www.grandtraverseballoons.com; 225 Cross Country Tr; $195-225
These eye-catching hot-air balloons carry a basket-load of passengers for a 15-mile panoramic tour at sunrise and sunset. If the winds are right, they'll take you for a truly spectacular trip across the Grand Traverse Bay that ends with a champagne celebration.

PARASAILING

Parasailing has become a popular activity, and it's an unusual summer afternoon if you don't see at least one parasail being towed around the bay. **Break 'n Waves** (☎ 231-929-3303, 888-504-2276; 1401 US 31 N; $60-75) is located in front of the Parkshore Resort and offers a 12-minute flight that goes up to 800ft in the air. When the boat is filled, you'll spend more than an hour cruising the bay.

THE GRAND TRAVERSE DINNER TRAIN

☎ 231-933-3768, 888-933-3768; www.dinnertrain.com; 642 Railroad Place; $75
Departing twice daily from an antique station downtown, this train winds 45 miles through Northern Michigan's scenic countryside while passengers enjoy a menu of four entrees prepared onboard.

MUSEUMS

Traverse City has a dozen museums for when the rain keeps you away from the beach. **The Music House** (☎ 231-938-9300; 7377 US 31 North; adult/child $8/2.50; ☼ 10am-4pm Mon-Sat, 12-4pm Sun May-Oct) is home to hundreds of pipe organs, nickelodeons and automatic musical machines from the 1880s through 1930. During the hourlong tours you listen to wax cylinders and watch a performance on a 30ft-high Belgian organ. The **Great Lakes Children's Museum** (☎ 231-932-4526; 336 W Front St; $5; ☼ 10am-5pm Tue-Sat, 1-5pm Sun-Mon) has more than 30 hands-on exhibits focusing on America's largest lakes. Kids can pilot a freighter, use a crane to load fish onto a vessel and learn about what lives under the surface.

The city's focal point of culture is the **Dennos Museum Center** (☎ 231-995-1055, 800-748-0566; 1701 E Front St; adults/kids $4/2; ☼ 10am-5pm Mon-Sat, 1-5pm Sun). Located at Northwestern Michigan College, the museum's signature collection is of Inuit art from Canada. It also has four other galleries and a children's hall with interactive exhibits.

SLEEPING

POINTES NORTH INN
☎ 231-938-9191, 800-968-3422; www.pointesnorth.com; 2211 US 31 North; d $100-275

This upscale resort has spacious rooms with Jacuzzis overlooking the bay and a private beach.

THE GREAT WOLF LODGE
☎ 231-941-3600, 866-GR8-WOLF; www.greatwolflodge.com; 3575 North US 31 South, ste $259-414

The indoor waterparks of the Wisconsin Dells have arrived in Michigan with this new four-story, log-sided lodge. Its 38,000-sq ft pool area includes eight waterslides, a 626ft-long tube slide and a giant bucket that dumps 1000 gallons of water at the sound of an alarm. Room rates include four passes to the waterpark.

MITCHELL CREEK INN
☎ 231-947-9330, 800-947-9330; www.mitchellecreek.com; 894 Munson Ave; d $55-60

Mitchell Creek Inn provides affordable lodging located directly across from Traverse City State Park's beach. Gurgling behind the inn is Mitchell Creek, where anglers cast for trout.

PARK SHORE RESORT
☎ 877-349-8898; www.parkshoreresort.com; 1401 US 31 North; d $160-260

This higher-end resort is on the bay, where guests can rent Jet Skis and water trampolines or enjoy bonfires at night. Amenities include whirlpool suites, an indoor pool, a lounge and free breakfast.

THE KNOLLWOOD MOTEL
☎ 231-938-2040; 5777 US 31; d $50-$80, cottages $55-$115; May-Oct

Nestled on the bay in Acme, this cheery motel has clean, bright rooms, small cottages and a private beach.

TRAVERSE CITY STATE PARK
☎ 231-922-5270; 1132 US 31; sites $23

This park is only 2 miles from downtown and has 343 modern sites on the east side of US 31, a beach on the west side and an elevated pedestrian walkway connecting them. Sites lack privacy, but the area is well shaded and connected to the TART Trail. **Reservations** (☎ 800-44-PARKS; www.michigan.gov/dnr) are a must.

EATING

DON'S DRIVE-IN
☎ 231-938-1860; 2030 US 31 North; mains $5-7; ⏲ 10:30am-10pm

When craving a hamburger, skip McDonald's and go to this classic, all-American diner. You can eat indoors, but if you stay outside, the wait staff will hang your tray from your car window, just like in the

'50s. Try the cherry shakes – so loaded with fruit that bits of cherries get stuck in your straw.

AMICAL
☎ 231-941-8888; 229 E Front St; mains $11-29; ☽ 11am-10pm Mon-Sat, 9am-10pm Sun

A trendy, mellow bistro with outside seating good for people-watching in the city's main shopping area, Amical offers an ample selection of appealing appetizers, salads and entrees like pasta and lamb. Finish your meal off with a fine French pastry.

TAQUERIA MARGARITA
☎ 231-935-3712; 1315 S Airport Rd; mains $6-9; ☽ 9am-9pm

Taqueria Margarita serves possibly the most authentic Mexican food in Northern Michigan. Top your chicken or chorizo tacos with cilantro, onion and lime for a savory meal.

APACHE TROUT AND GRILL
☎ 231-947-7079; 13671 W Bay Shore Dr; mains $7-17; ☽ 11am-11pm Mon-Sat, 12-10pm Sun

Away from the main hustle of Traverse City, this restaurant has a deck overlooking the bay and a relaxed atmosphere. Entrees range from tequila-lime-chicken pasta to sautéed rainbow trout.

NORTH PEAK BREWING COMPANY
☎ 231-941-PEAK; 400 W Front St; mains $11-13; ☽ 11am-12am Mon-Thu, 11am-1am Fri-Sat, 12-10pm Sun

Housed in an old brick warehouse and featuring outside dining, this microbrewery serves a variety of salads, gourmet pizzas, sandwiches and, of course, cold pints of handcrafted beer. For those who don't drink alcohol, the brewery also makes delicious root beer.

TRILLIUM RESTAURANT
☎ 231-938-2100, 800-748-0303; www.grandtraverseresort.com; 100 Grand Traverse Village Blvd (off of US 31 in Acme); buffet $16, ☽ 10:30am-2pm Sun

No one does Sunday brunch better then this restaurant at the upscale Grand Traverse Resort. Nor does any restaurant have a better view than what you see from your table on the 17th floor.

ENTERTAINMENT & SHOPPING

Being larger has its benefits, including a more energetic nightlife than any other Northern Michigan city. The center of Traverse City's nightlife is on Union St, where the **Union Street Station** (☎ 231-941-1930; 117 S Union St; ☽ 11:30am-2am) has hosted many Detroit rockers. Next door are two connecting pubs called **Bootleggers** (☎ 231-922-7742; 119 S Union St; ☽ 11am-2am) and **Dillingers Pub** (☎ 231-941-2276; 121 S Union S; ☽ 11am-2am Mon-Sat, 12pm-2am Sun). For jazz fans there is **Poppycock's** (☎ 231-941-7632; 128 E Front St; ☽ 11am-10pm Mon-Tue, 11am-12am Wed-Sat, 12-9pm Sun), where local jazz artists do improv jams on the weekends. For more jazz, head to Mission Peninsula's **Chateau Chantal** (☎ 800-969-4009; 15900 Rue de Vin), where the Jeff Haas Trio takes over the tasting room every Thursday at 7pm for Jazz at Sunset. For dancing, **Streeters** (☎ 231-932-1300; 1669 S Garfield Ave; ☺ opens 4pm Tue-Sat, 6pm Sun) features four distinct clubs in the same building. Concerts and classical music are enjoyed at **Interlochen Center for the Arts** (☎ 800-681-5920; http://tickets.interlochen.org; 4000 MI 137, Interlochen), 16 miles southwest of Traverse City. The famed music camp hosts guest artists from June through November; guests have included everyone from the Boston Pops to Lyle Lovett.

Front St is considered downtown. It's a busy area lined with gift shops, clothing boutiques and outdoor cafés. If you're tired of souvenir shops, **Grand Traverse Mall** (☎ 231-922-7722; 3200 S Airport Rd W) has the usual chain stores.

OLD MISSION PENINSULA

Extending from Traverse City is this 20-mile-long finger of gently rolling cherry orchards and vineyards overlooking the glistening East and West Arms of the Grand Traverse Bay. First settled in 1839 when Rev Peter Dougherty arrived to set up a mission, the peninsula is now a favorite for scenic drives and long bicycle rides.

SIGHTS & ACTIVITIES

VINEYARDS
The location and shape of the peninsula provides the ideal climate for growing grapes, and several wineries have sprung up in the area, growing and bottling Chardonnay, Riesling, Pinot Grigio and Pinot Noir. The first vineyard was **Chateau Grand Traverse** (☎ 231-223-7355; 12239 Center Rd; ☺ 10am-7pm Mon-Sat, 12-6pm Sun). Just up M-37 on the highest point of the peninsula is **Chateau Chantel** (☎ 231-223-4110; 15900 Rue de Vin; ☺ 11am-8pm Mon-Sat, 12-5pm Sun). At **Peninsula Cellars** (☎ 231-933-9787; 11480 Center Rd; ☺ 10am-6pm Mon-Sat, 12-6pm Sun May-Oct), you can sip its dry white wines in a renovated, century-old red-and-white schoolhouse that now serves as a sampling room.

PENINSULA TOWNSHIP PARK
This lovely, 500-acre park lies on the 45th parallel – halfway between the equator and the North Pole – at the end of MI 37. Within the park is an 1870 lighthouse, picnic area, cobbled stone beaches and 3 miles of hiking trails through the woods – a great place to enjoy that bottle of wine you just bought at the vineyard.

OLD MISSION CHURCH
Old Mission Rd; ☺ 9am-6pm May-Oct
This small museum of local history is a replica of an 1839 log church

built by the Presbyterian missionary. Particularly interesting is the exhibit on the impact of the cherry industry on the peninsula.

SLEEPING & EATING

OLD MISSION TAVERN
☎ 231-223-7280; 17015 Center Rd; mains $7-30; ✆ 11:30am-3pm, 5-9pm
Old Mission Tavern is a cozy yet elegant restaurant serving dishes like king crab and chicken artichoke. The walls of the tavern double as a gallery for local artists.

BOWERS HARBOR INN
☎ 231-223-4222; 13512 Peninsula Dr; mains $20-30; ✆ 5-10pm Sun-Thu, 5-11pm Fri-Sat
They say this historic inn is haunted by the original owner's wife. No doubt her spirit is hanging around to savor such engaging dishes as mint pesto-glazed lamb chops. This is one of the most highly recommended restaurants in the Grand Traverse region; reservations are a must.

THE BOWERY
☎ 231-223-4222; 13512 Peninsula Dr; mains $8-17; ✆ 4-10pm Sun-Thu, 4-11pm Fri-Sat
Located in the back of the Bowers Harbor Inn is her more affordable sister, a publike restaurant serving sandwiches, salads and lighter fare.

CHATEAU CHANTAL VINEYARD
☎ 800-969-4009; www.chateauchantal.com; 15900 Rue de Vin; d $135-185
This European-style winery offers the unique experience of staying at a vineyard in a beautiful hilltop inn. The vineyard has 11 rooms, eight of them suites with private decks overlooking the rows of grapes.

ON THE ROAD

It's a 50-mile drive from Traverse City to Charlevoix along US 31. You rarely see Lake Michigan and pass through only one town of any significance along this route, but this is still an interesting stretch, because it passes through cherry country. From mid-July to mid-August, you'll see orchards laden with fruit, workers shaking cherries off the trees and a dozen roadside stands selling everything from sweet cherries and cherry pie to cherry jam and juice. Buy a quart of sweet giant blacks ($3-4), and you'll be popping them into your mouth like jelly beans on Easter morning and spitting the pits out the car window all the way to Charlevoix.

Fifteen miles from Traverse City is **Elk Rapids** (pop 1700), the only town of any size until Charlevoix. Founded in 1848, only a year after Traverse City, Elk Rapids is surrounded by Lake Michigan, Elk Lake and Bass Lake and split in half by Elk River. The beach at **Veterans Memorial Park** on River St is as nice as any in Traverse

City but never as crowded. There are also a handful of gift and antique shops and a surprising number of good restaurants for such a small town. Try **Pearl's** (☎ 231-264-0530; 617 Ames St; mains $9-21, ☟ 11am-11pm Mon-Sat, 10am-10pm Sun) for Cajun dishes and hush puppies or **Fish & Bonz Café** (☎ 231-264-8944; 145 Ames St; mains $7-15; ☟ 6:30am-8pm Mon-Sat) for ribs and pulled-pork sandwiches. On Elk Lake is **White Birch Lodge** (☎ 231-264-8271; www.whitebirchlodge.org; 571 Meguzee Point Rd; $875-1200 per person per week) an all-inclusive resort with a minimum seven-day stay during the summer that offers lots of activities, including waterskiing.

In another 11 miles is **Peterson's 31 North Restaurant** (☎ 231-599-3130; 3910 N US 31, Torch Lake; mains $9-20; ☟ 5-8pm Mon-Thu, 5-10pm Fri-Sun), a roadhouse with a fireplace in the main room and an excellent perch fry on Friday. Come hungry – the portions are huge. **Friske Orchards** (☎ 231-599-2604; www.friske.com; 10743 US 31, Atwood; ☟ 8am-7pm Mon-Sat May-Oct), 18 miles from Elk Rpaids, is a large farmers market with an orchard playground for the kids and opportunities to pick cherries in July. US 31 passes several art galleries and antique shops, including **Bier Art Gallery** (231-547-2288; www.biergallery.com; 03500 US 31; ☟ 10am-6pm Mon-Sun) housed in a red, century-old schoolhouse. This gallery sells works from local and national artists and has a ceramics studio upstairs.

Five miles south of Charlevoix is **Fisherman's Island State Park** (☎ 231-547-6641, Bells Bay Rd; vehicle $6, site $10). This 2678-acre park is one of the most unusual units along Lake Michigan and includes 2.5 miles of undeveloped shoreline. Petoskey-stone hunting is so popular, they have how-to information at the campground office. Fisherman's Island has 90 rustic sites with a handful right on a sandy stretch of Lake Michigan.

CHARLEVOIX

Population 3116; Map 4

This attractive town is nestled between Lake Michigan and Lake Charlevoix and in the summer is transformed into an affluent place of beaches, boating and boutiques. The **Charlevoix Chamber of Commerce** (☎ 231-547-2101; www.charlevoix.org; 408 Bridge St; ☟ 9am-5pm Mon-Sat) has ample information for tourists.

SIGHTS & ACTIVITIES

WALKING TOUR

Take a self-guided architectural tour of 30 downtown buildings designed in the 1920s by famed architect and local resident **Earl Young**. Locals call these buildings 'mushroom houses' because their large boulder facades and rounded tops give them a fairy-tale quality. Pick up a tour brochure at the chamber of commerce.

SUNSHINE CHARTERS
☎ 231-547-0266; www.sunshinecharters.com; 408 Bridge St

Boating, naturally, is an extremely popular activity in Charlevoix. Even you if you didn't bring your own vessel, you can still enjoy the water. Sunshine Charters has three sailing tours a day in its 45ft sailboat on either Lake Michigan or Lake Charlevoix, depending on the conditions. The two-hour trips are $30/20 adult/child, and tickets can be purchased at a kiosk across from Charlevoix City Dock No 32.

SWIMMING
There are five public beaches in the area. The warmer water is in Lake Charlevoix at **Ferry Beach** (Ferry Ave and Stover Rd) and **Depot Beach** (Coast Guard Dr and Chicago St). For bigger surf, head to **Lake Michigan Park** (Park Ave and Grant St) on Lake Michigan.

CYCLING
Lake Charlevoix is a popular 32-mile ride for cyclists, who begin by heading north on the **Little Traverse Wheelway** along US 31. Turn off on Boyne City Rd for Boyne City and then follow Ferry Rd to Ironton, where you hop on the **Ironton Ferry** to cross the south arm of the lake. You return to Charlevoix via MI 66. The highlight for many cyclists is stopping at Horton Bay, where Ernest Hemingway spent his summers as a youth (see **Touring Hemingway Country**, p53). The closest place to rent a bicycle is in Petoskey.

SLEEPING & EATING

VILLA MODERNE MOTEL
☎ 231-547-2578, 888-844-2578; 1415 Bridge St; d $45-$80

One of the more affordable accommodations in town, this motel has clean country-style rooms with patchwork quilts and rocking chairs.

WEATHERVANE TERRACE INN
☎ 231-547-9955, 800-552-0025; www.weathervane-chx.com; 111 Pine River Lane; d $119-269

Noted architect Earl Young designed this hotel with stone walls and cylinder towers. The rooms are comfortable (some suites include Jacuzzis and kitchenettes), but the high price is due primarily to its location, right downtown overlooking the channel to Lake Michigan.

EDGEWATER INN
☎ 231-547-6044, 800-748-0424; www.edgewater-charlevoix.com; 100 Michigan Ave; d $185-255

This condominium hotel has one- and two-room suites that are spacious and modern. They come with kitchens, living rooms, balconies and views of either the channel or city harbor on Round Lake.

BRIDGE STREET INN
☎ 231-547-6606; www.bridgestreetinn-chx.com; 113 Michigan Ave, $90-145

This three-story Colonial Revival home was built in 1895, but it's been well maintained and is not nearly as gaudy as other Victorian B&Bs in the area. If the weather is nice, breakfast is served on the long porch, which offers splendid views of Lake Michigan.

JUILLERET'S
☎ 231-547-9212; 1418 Bridge St; mains $4-10; ☽ 7am-3pm
One of the best places in town for breakfast, Juilleret's serves great cinnamon French toast and raspberry pancakes. Lunch is also served.

THE ACORN CAFÉ
☎ 231-547-1835; 103 Park Ave; mains $6-9; ☽ 7am-3pm
Its sign claims that Hemingway never ate here. The writer definitely missed out by not dining in this charming café, which puts a unique twist on traditional breakfast and lunch dishes.

WHITNEY'S OYSTER BAR
☎ 231-547-0818; 307 Bridge St; mains $7-22; ☽ 11:30am-11pm
This lively bar and restaurant has outdoor seating, rooftop entertainment in June and July and decor that makes you feel like you are drinking with fishermen in New England. Naturally, Whitney's is the place to head for seafood, including good oyster stew.

ENTERTAINMENT & SHOPPING

Shopping in Charlevoix is as upscale as Petoskey and Harbor Springs. Many of the art galleries and clothing boutiques are located on Bridge St. There is also a good collection of antique stores, such as **Don Kelly's Antiques** (☎ 231-547-0133; 06176 US 31 S; ☽ 8am-4pm Mon-Sat, 8am-1pm Sun), known for its vintage cottage furniture.

The Village Pub (☎ 231-547-6925, 427 Bridge St; ☽ opens 11am) hops with bands and dancing Thursday through Saturday. There are weekly concerts in **East Park** (☽ 8pm Thu Jun-Aug) featuring a variety of music ranging from jazz to steel drum.

Charlevoix hosts two annual art fairs, the **Charlevoix Craft Show** in mid-July and the **Waterfront Art Fair** on the second Saturday of August, when the downtown area is filled with several hundred artisans. The city's longest running event is the **Venetian Festival** on the fourth weekend in July, when there is music, food, fireworks and a parade of boats on Round Lake.

ON THE ROAD

It's 16 miles from Charlevoix to Petoskey along US 31, a very scenic drive that hugs Little Traverse Bay practically the entire way. On the north edge of Charlevoix, at the corner of Waller Rd and US 31, the **Little Traverse Wheelway** begins. This 29-mile paved path was completed in 2004 and provides cyclists with a smooth and safe route all the way to Petoskey and Harbor Springs. It's one of

DETOUR: BEAVER ISLAND

With its bizarre history and tranquil, beautiful setting, Beaver Island makes for an interesting side trip either for a day or overnight. At 53 sq miles, it's one of the largest islands in the Great Lakes, and the vast majority of it is forests, inland lakes and undeveloped shoreline. Unlike Mackinac Island, Beaver Island isn't spoiled by swarms of tourists and fudge shops. You reach the island from Charlevoix by the **Beaver Island Boat Co** (☎ 888-446-4095; www.bibco. com; 103 Bridge Park Dr, Charlevoix; adult/child roundtrip $35/17). For more information, contact the **Beaver Island Chamber of Commerce** (☎ 231-448-2505; www.beaverisland.net; 26180 Main St, St James; ⏰ 8:30am-4pm Mon-Fri).

Islanders love to brag that Beaver Island was the country's only kingdom. In 1847, James Jesse Strang broke away from Brigham Young and the rest of the Mormons and arrived at the island with his own followers. They founded **St James**, the island's only village, and eventually Strang crowned himself 'King of Beaver Island.' He ruled the island with an iron hand before being assassinated in 1856. Irish immigrants arrived next to establish a fishery, and today Beaver Island is known as the Emerald Isle for its strong Irish heritage.

In St James there are several museums, including the **Old Mormon Print Shop** (☎ 231-448-2254; 26275 Main St; adult/child $3/1.50; ⏰ 11am-5pm Mon-Sat, 12-3pm Sun), which was built by King Strand, and the **Marine Museum** (no ☎ ; Main St; adult/child $3/1.50; ⏰ 11am-5pm Mon-Sat, 12-3pm Sun), a 1906 net shed dedicated to the time when the area bustled with fishermen. There is also the playful **Toy Museum and Store** (☎ 231-448-2480; 37970 Michigan Ave; ⏰ 11am-4pm Mon-Sun), which was once known as 'the last nickel store in the US.' It's still affordable to anybody on a weekly allowance. Suspended from the ceiling is a collection of antique toys ranging from the 1930s rocket cars to dolls that predate the 1900s.

To explore the island, rent a car from **Gordon's Auto Clinic** (☎ 231-448-2438; 175 Lake Dr, St James; $55 a day) or a mountain bike from **Lakesports Rental** (☎ 231-448-2166; 26250 Main St, St James; $20 a day). Most of the 100 miles of roads are dirt – excellent for mountain biking – and pass old farmhouses, two lighthouses and beaches without a soul on them.

To spend the night there, camp at **Bill Wagner Memorial Campground** (East Side Dr; site $10) 1.5 miles south of St James on beautiful Big Sand Bay. Or try one the island's motels, cabins or B&Bs. The newest is the **Emerald Isle Hotel** (☎ 231-448-2376; www.emeraldislehotel.com; 37985 Kings Hwy; d $99-115, suites $142-159), which opened in 2000.

the most beautiful bike paths in Michigan and at times is so close to the shoreline that boulders had to be piled up along the path to protect it from the heavy surf generated by storms. You can rent bicycles at a number of shops in Harbor Springs and Petoskey, including **Bahnhof Sports** (☎ 231-347-2112; 1300 Bay View Rd; ⏰ 9am-8pm) for $25 a day.

Within 10 miles US 31 begins skirting the sprawling **Bay Harbor Resort**, a complex of three 18-hole golf courses surrounded by homes and condos, an equestrian club and its own shopping area with restaurants and bars. The very upscale **Inn at Bay Harbor** (☎ 231-439-4000; www.innatbayharbor.com; 3600 Village Harbor Dr; d $300-430) is a Victorian-inspired hotel within the resort and has 85 suites and 24 lakeside cottages.

PETOSKEY & HARBOR SPRINGS

Population: Petoskey 6056, Harbor Springs 1544; Map 8

For more than a century, Michigan's upper crust has made this area the location of their summer homes. Both towns are tucked deep into Little Traverse Bay and are adorned with boutiques, colorful Victorian cottages, well-maintained parks and beaches. Petoskey is by far the larger of the two towns and more geared towards tourists.

For information there's **Petoskey Visitors and Convention Bureau** (☎ 800-845-2828; www.boynecountry.com; 401 E Mitchell St; ☉ 8am-4pm).

SIGHTS & ACTIVITIES

LITTLE TRAVERSE HISTORY MUSEUM
☎ 231-347-2620; www.petoskeymuseum.org; adult/child $1/free; ☉ 10am-4pm Mon-Fri, 1-4pm Sat

Overlooking Petoskey's waterfront, this museum is housed in the restored Pere Marquette Railroad Depot. Exhibits include Odawa tribal artifacts, autographed copies of Ernest Hemingway's books and tools from the city's early logging days.

BAY VIEW
A national historic landmark east of Petoskey, this Victorian community consists of 440 elegant cottages laced in gingerbread trim and painted in vivid colors. Bay View was founded in 1875 by the Methodist church as a summer retreat and still maintains a renowned music and theater camp that stages concerts, operas and plays throughout the summer. For tickets and a schedule contact the **Bay View Association** (☎ 231-347-6225; www.bayviewassoc.com).

HISTORIC TOURS
For a 90-minute tour of Petoskey, **Historic Trolley Tours** (☎ 231-347-4000; adult/child $10/5; 10:30am Thu & Fri) leave from the Perry Hotel (100 Lewis St) downtown. **Bay Breeze Tours** (☎ 231-526-8888; www.northquest.com/baybreeze; adult/child $12/5; Jul-Aug) offers hour-long walking tours of Bay View that depart at 1pm from the Terrace Inn (1549 Glendale St) on Wednesdays and Stafford's Bay View Inn (2011 Woodland Ave) on Thursdays.

PETOSKEY STATE PARK
☎ 231-347-2311; 2475 M-119; vehicle $6, site $23

Located between Petoskey and Harbor Springs, this 304-acre park has a beautiful beach loaded with Petoskey stones. Away from the bay, there are forested dunes laced by 3.5-miles of trails. The park also features 170 modern sites and is virtually filled nightly in the summer Call for **reservations** (☎ 800-44-PARKS; www.michigan.gov/dnr).

ANDREW BLACKBIRD MUSEUM
☎ 231-526-0612; 368 E Main St, Harbor Springs; 10am-4pm Mon-Fri, ☽ 10am-2pm Sat; admission free

The first post office of Harbor Springs has been converted into a museum focusing on Native American customs, arts, crafts, music and poetry. During the 1840s this area had Michigan's largest concentration of Native Americans.

SLEEPING

MAGNUS CITY PARK
☎ 231-347-1027; 101 E Lake St; sites $15-19

Overlooking the Little Traverse Bay, this park has 80 sites, including 68 with full hookups, making it probably the cheapest place to stay in Petoskey.

LITTLE TRAVERSE BAY INN
☎ 231-347-2593, 888-321-2500; www.littletraversebayinn.com; 2445 Charlevoix Ave (US 31) Petoskey; d $49-119

This inviting inn has 15 comfortable rooms, each with patios for enjoying the view of Lake Michigan.

STAFFORD'S BAY VIEW INN
☎ 231-347-2771, 800-258-1886; www.thebayviewinn.com; 2011 Woodland Ave, Bay View; d $89-280 includes breakfast

One of two places to stay in Bay View, this historic inn offers access to a beach on the bay. It has both rooms and suites and one of the finest restaurants in the area.

TERRACE INN
☎ 231-347-2410, 800-530-9898; www.theterraceinn.com; 1549 Glendale St, Bay View; d $79-109 includes breakfast

Located among the Victorian cottages of Bay View, Terrace Inn is often called the 'Little Grand Hotel.' Outside there is a pleasant veranda; inside there is a fine restaurant and rooms with themes such as *Lighthouse Lovers* and *Hemingway*.

BIRCHWOOD INN
☎ 231-526-2151; www.birchwoodinn.com; 7077 Lake Shore Dr, Harbor Springs; d $70-155 includes breakfast

North of Harbor Springs along MI 119 (the 'Tunnel of Trees' drive) is this inn, which offers a variety of rooms and an outdoor pool and hot tub. Every spring and fall Birchwood Inn stages organized bicycle rides along MI 119.

NICK ADAMS HOTEL
☎ 800-526-6238; www.nickadamshotel.com; 266 E Main St, Harbor Springs; d $195-285

This boutique hotel has a great location in the middle of Harbor Springs with views of the bay – the reason, no doubt, for its high room rates.

EATING

ANDANTE
☎ 231-348-3321; 321 Bay St, Petoskey; mains $39-48; 5:30-9pm, Tue-Sun

Located in an historic townhouse, this restaurant serves innovative dishes from a menu blending regional, Asian and European fare.

WHITECAPS
☎ 231-348-7092; www.whitecapsrestaurant.com; 215 E Lake St, Petoskey; mains $14-30; 11am-10pm

Whitecaps is one of the few restaurants overlooking Little Traverse Bay. This upscale establishment has a contemporary menu featuring dishes such as whitefish grenoble and slow-roasted prime rib.

ROAST & TOAST CAFÉ
☎ 231-347-7767; 309 E Lake St, Petoskey; sandwiches $5-6; 7am-9pm

This espresso shop and bakery, with a distinct coffee cup mosaic doorway, roasts its own beans on site and is a good place for affordable sandwiches and salads.

THE FISH
☎ 231-526-3969; 2983 S State Rd; Harbor Springs; mains $23-38; 4-10pm Mon-Sat, 10:30am-2:30pm Sun

This lively seafood restaurant serves freshwater fish and seafood, like herb-crusted walleye and Caribbean scallops. It's also open for Sunday brunch.

GURNEY'S LIQUOR STORE
☎ 231-526-5472; 215 E Main St, Harbor Springs; sandwiches $4-6; 9am-6pm Mon-Sat

Gurney's is a local favorite for fresh deli sandwiches on thick, soft bread. Buy a bottle of wine and a sandwich, then head to the harbor for a picnic.

SHOPPING & ENTERTAINMENT

In the late 1800s a number of shops sprang up to cater to affluent resorters and formed what is now known as the **Gaslight District** in downtown Petoskey. This part of town is still bustling with shoppers exploring gift shops and intriguing art galleries like the

Gaslight Gallery (☎ 866-348-5079; 200 Howard St; 10am-9pm). Also in the Gaslight District is **Symon's General Store** (☎ 231-347-2438; 401 E Lake St; 8am-8pm), a classic general store stocked with a variety of cheese and brie, fresh-baked breads, regional wine and, of course, penny candy. Nearby, **American Spoon Foods** (☎ 231-347-9030; 1668 Clarion Ave; 10am-5pm Mon-Sat, 12-4pm Sun), sells and ships its large selection of preserves, salsas and fruit butters all over the country.

Petoskey is a lively little town at night, and one of its best pubs is the **Noggin Room** (☎ 231-347-4000; 100 Lewis St; 11:30am-11pm Mon-Wed, 11:30am-12am Thu-Sat, 12-10pm Sun) downstairs in the Perry Hotel. This bar has pub food, a wide selection of beers and entertainment Wednesday through Saturday. The **City Park Grill** (☎ 231-347-0101; 432 E Lake Rd; 11:30am-12am Sun-Wed, 11:30am-2am Thu-Sat) also has live entertainment and a comedy night every other Thursday. Reputedly Ernest Hemingway drank at both places. South of town is **Victories Casino** (☎ 877-442-6464; 1967 US 131; 8am-4am) which has 850 slot machines, table games, a restaurant and often live entertainment.

ON THE ROAD

North of Harbor Springs MI 119 is a scenic route known as the **Tunnel of Trees Shoreline Drive**. It's a narrow road that climbs, dips and curves its way through thick forests and along steep bluffs. At times, the trees on each side of the road merge overhead to form a leafy tunnel. Within 14 miles you pass through **Good Hart**, where you can enjoy deli sandwiches at picturesque **Good Hart Store** (☎ 231-526-7661; 1075 N Lake Shore Dr; 10am-6pm Mon-Sat,

Touring Hemingway Country

Many writers have ties to northwest Michigan, but none are more famous than Ernest Hemingway, who spent his childhood summers at his family's cottage on Walloon Lake. Hemingway buffs gather every fall for a weekend hosted by the **Michigan Hemingway Society** (www.northquest.com/hemingway; PO Box 953, Petoskey, MI 49770) to tour the area and places that made their way into his writing. In Petoskey they view the Hemingway collection at the **Little Traverse History Museum** (p50) and visit one of several bars in town, such as the **City Park Grill** (☎ 231-347-0101; 432 E Lake St) where the author, with his infamous drinking habit, was a regular. Eventually they journey west on US 31 and then south on Boyne City Rd to tiny Horton Bay on Lake Charlevoix. Hemingway idled away youthful summers on the large front porch of **Horton Bay General Store** (☎ 231-582-7827; 05115 Boyne City Rd; 7am-6pm Mon-Thu, 7am-8pm Fri-Sat, 7am-4pm Sun) and later used this classic country store in the opening of his short story *Up in Michigan*.

10am-5pm Sun). Continuing 7 miles north, you emerge from the thick forest at **Cross Village**, home of **Legs Inn** (☎ 231-526-2281; 6425 S Lakeshore Dr; mains $10-15; ☺ 11am-10pm May-Oct), a renowned Polish restaurant filled with driftwood that has been carved into everything imaginable. Here you can indulge in pierogi, Polish beer and a view of Lake Michigan all at the same time.

From Cross Village, continue north on Lake Shore Dr for 6.5 miles to reach **Bliss Township Park**, a wonderful, undeveloped beach whose only amenity is a cement bathhouse. Keep heading north on Lake Shore Dr, which becomes Lakeview Rd in 2 miles and then swings east to pass a trailhead for the **North Country Trail**. To the north, the national trail winds through Wilderness State Park; to the south, it climbs rugged hills on its way to Wycamp Lake. Continue west on Lakeview Rd as it turns into Gill Rd and in 3 miles arrives at County Rd C81. To the north C81 leads to **Mackinaw City** and within 4 miles passes Wilderness Park Dr, which heads west for Wilderness State Park.

WILDERNESS STATE PARK

Long beaches and a backcountry that gives credence to its name are the outstanding features of **Wilderness State Park** (☎ 231-436-5381; 903 Wilderness Park Dr, Carp Lake; vehicle $6, site $23), the second largest state park in the Lower Peninsula. Located 11 miles west of Mackinaw City, the park attracts more than 170,000 visitors annually, but with 8,286 acres and 30 miles of shoreline you can easily escape the crowds.

ACTIVITIES

SWIMMING

Wilderness State Park has a day-use area on **Big Stone Bay**, which includes a beautiful beach where you can swim within view of the Mackinac Bridge.

HIKING & MOUNTAIN BIKING

The park has 20 miles of designated foot trails, including a segment of the **North Country Trail**, the national trail from North Dakota to New York. The **Sturgeon Bay Trail**, the longest trail in the park, can be combined with the **Swamp Trail** (bring your bug spray!) to form a 5-mile loop through the park.

There are also 11 miles of two tracks opened for mountain biking that make for easy, nontechnical riding. You can rent mountain bikes for $25 a day in Petoskey at **Bahnhof Sports** (p49).

KAYAKING

In recent years kayaking has become popular in the park, with kayakers paddling around **Waugoshance Point** and **Crane** and **Temperance**

Islands. Rent kayaks at **Bahnhof Sports** in Petoskey for $35 a day for singles and $50 for doubles.

SLEEPING

CAMPING
The park has 250 modern sites divided between two campgrounds. The **Lakeshore Campground** is situated along Big Stone Bay and has a row of sites right off the beach. **Pines Campground** is more inland and has 100 sites, most of them in a grove of mature pines. Both campgrounds tend to be filled most summer weekends but usually have sites available midweek; call for **reservations** (☎ 800-44-PARKS; www.michigan.gov/dnr).

CABINS
There are six rustic **cabins** ($55 a night) scattered throughout the park that offer an opportunity of a quiet night in the backcountry. The best and most isolated ones are **Sturgeon Cabin** on Sturgeon Bay and **Nebo Cabin** reached by a 2-mile hike. Cabins are rented in advance through the **park headquarters** (☎ 231-436-5381).

MACKINAW CITY

Population 900; Map 4
Mackinaw City is at the south end of the Mackinaw Bridge, overlooking the Straits of Mackinac. This town seems to have a fudge stand on every corner. Look beyond the tacky tourist shops, though, and you'll find several interesting attractions that make Mackinaw City worth a visit. The city's long history began in 1715, when the fur-trading French built a fort here that was later occupied by the British. For travel information, stop at the **Mackinaw Area Tourist Bureau** (☎ 800-666-0160; www.mackinawcity.com; 10300 S US 23; ☽ 8am-7pm Mon-Fri, 9am-1pm Sat).

SIGHTS & ACTIVITIES

FORT MICHILIMACKINAC
☎ 231-436-4100; www.mackinacparks.com; Huron St; adult/child $9/5.75, ☽ 9am-6pm May-Oct
A reconstructed 1715 fort and colonial village comes to life with British redcoats firing cannons and muskets, colonial wives cooking over open hearths and French voyageurs arriving in fur-loaded canoes. The dozen buildings inside the fort are staffed by guides who demonstrate a slice of colonial life.

OLD MACKINAC POINT LIGHTHOUSE
☎ 231-436-4100; www.mackinacparks.com; Huron St; adult/child $5/3, ☽ 9am-5pm Jun-Oct
This Victorian brick lighthouse protected sailors on the straits from

1892 until 1957, when the Mackinaw Bridge opened with better navigation signals. Along with panoramic views of the bridge and two Great Lakes from the top of its tower, the museum offers interactive exhibits and tours by guides dressed as lightkeepers.

MACKINAW CITY HISTORIC PATH
Learn Mackinaw City's colorful history with a walk along this a 2.2-mile loop that begins in Conking Heritage Park on South Huron Rd. The path includes more than 40 interpretive displays covering everything from the first shipwreck in the Great Lakes to an ill-fated plan in the 1800s to build a bridge to Mackinac Island.

STRAITS OF MACKINAC LIGHTHOUSE CRUISES
☎ 800-828-6157; www.sheplersferry.com; 556 E Central Ave; $49.50; ⏰ 1:30pm various days Jun-Sep
Shepler's Ferry offers three-hour tours to the numerous lighthouses in the region. The boat pulls within 20 yards of some of them while providing insights about shipwrecks, navigation methods and the light keepers who lived in the middle of nowhere. Even for people who aren't lighthouse fanatics, these cruises are a pleasant way to see the straits.

SLEEPING & EATING

PARKSIDE INN
☎ 231-436-8301, 800-827-8301; www.parksideinn.com; 771 N Huron St, d $108-128
Mackinaw City has a number of upscale resorts and hotels, but it's hard to pass up the location of the Parkside. It's just off exit 339, right across from the entrance to Fort Michilimackinac. The inn has the largest indoor pool in the city and offers guests free breakfast and van transportation to the ferry boats.

BRIGADOON B&B
☎ 231-436-8882; www.mackinawbrigadoon.com; 207 Langlade St; ste $125-295
Located just a block from the shops of Central Avenue, this enchanting B&B has eight suites and looks like it belongs on Mackinac Island rather than among the national chains of Mackinaw City.

VINDEL MOTEL
☎ 231-436-5273, 800-968-5273; www.vindelmotel.com; 223 W Central Ave; d $46-82
On the west side of I-75 just off exit 339 are several economical motels. The Vindel offers the cleanest rooms, along with a small outdoor pool.

MAMA MIA PIZZERIA
☎ 231-436-5534; 231 Central Ave.; pizza $11-17; ⏰ 8am-12am
JC Stilwell was one of the 2000 men that built the Mackinac Bridge, and in 1980 he opened this pizzeria. He turned the top floor into the Mackinaw Bridge Museum and filled it with photos and artifacts

donated by his former coworkers. Downstairs there are more than 1000 hard hats hanging on the walls. The pizza is good and the museum is free.

AUDIE'S
☎ 231-436-5744; 314 N Nicolet St; breakfast $4-$8, mains $6-10; ☷ 8am-10pm
Audie's is a local favorite for breakfast, offering such dishes as broiled whitefish with eggs and 'secret formula' pancakes. Lunch and dinner are also served.

DIXIE SALOON
☎ 231-436-5005; 401 E Central Ave; mains $7-20; ☷ 11am-1:30am May-Oct
This is a large double-floor saloon with the rustic wood interior of a sawmill. On the menu are big burgers, sandwiches, ribs and steak, while on tap is a nice selection of beer.

ENTERTAINMENT & SHOPPING

Central Ave is lined with shops and restaurants and serves as the downtown area for Mackinaw City. Also along Central Ave and Shepler's Dr are the entrances to **Mackinaw Crossings** (☎ 231-436-5030; www.mackinawcrossings.com; 248 S Huron Ave; ☷ 10am-10pm May-Oct). This enclave of 50 shops and six restaurants is spread over 7 acres and often overrun with tour bus groups. But the complex is pedestrian-only and makes a nice place to hang out while waiting for the next ferry to Mackinac Island.

The **Dixie Saloon** hops nightly while at Mackinaw Crossing there is an outdoor laser light show (free; dusk May-Oct). **Mackinaw Center Stage Theatre** (☎ 877-43-STAGE; www.mackinawcenterstagetheatre.com; May-Oct) hosts live productions. Or head to Conkling Heritage Park on South Huron Rd for the local outdoor concert **Music of Mackinaw** (free; ☷ 8pm Thu-Sat Jul-Aug).

ON THE FERRY

Leave your car behind for a trip to **Mackinac Island**, which banned automobiles in the 1920s, making it a paradise for cyclists ever since. Three passenger ferry lines service the island, departing from either St Igance and Mackinaw City; **Arnold Line** (☎ 800-542-8528; www.arnoldline.com), **Shepler's** (☎ 800-828-6157; www.sheplersferry.com) and **Star Line** (☎ 800-638-9892; www.mackinacferry.com).

No matter where you depart from or which ferry you choose, the roundtrip fare is the same (adult/child $17/8). So much for free enterprise. Shepler's and Star Line offer free parking. Arnold Line's parking fee ranges from $1 for an outside lot to $15 for valet indoor parking. Keep in mind it's another $6.50 for your bike and $2.50 to cross the Mackinac Bridge if you choose to leave from St Igance.

MACKINAC ISLAND

Population 400; Map 1

This 3-mile-long island is considered the jewel of the Great Lakes and one of Michigan's best-known tourist destinations. It's a place where a colorful history and natural beauty has been carefully preserved, and horse-drawn taxis still clip-clop down streets lined with Victorian cottages.

Native Americans were using the island as a summer fish camp when the British arrived in 1780 to build Fort Mackinac. They gave the fort to the Americans following the Revolutionary War and then recaptured it in one of the first battles of the War of 1812. Tourists descended on Mackinac Island following the Civil War and in 1875, only three years after Yellowstone was established, the island became the country's second national park. Later it was redesignated as Michigan's first state park.

The following listings are all open daily May to October. Peak season on the island is late June through August, when the downtown area is often packed with tourists, horses and bicycles. For a more relaxing trip, avoid the weekends or plan to stay the night. It's amazing how the empty the streets become after the last ferries depart for the day. Even better is to visit in May or September. For help finding a room, the **Mackinac Island Chamber of Commerce** (☎ 906-847-6418, 800-454-5227; www.mackinacisland.org; Huron St; ⏱ 9am-7pm Mon-Sat, 9am-5pm Sun) maintains a kiosk across from Arnold's Ferry.

SIGHTS & ACTIVITIES

FORT MACKINAC
☎ 906-847-3328; Fort St; adult/child $9/5.75; ⏱ 9:30am-6pm

Overlooking the downtown area is one of the best-preserved military forts in the country. Explore its 14 original buildings, listen to guides in period costumes explain military life during the 1800s and watch rifle and cannon demonstrations. The ticket is also your pass to six other museums in town including **Indian Dormitory**, **Beaumont Memorial** and **Benjamin Blacksmith Shop**. For information about the fort and the park once you're on the island visit the **Mackinac State Historic Parks Visitor's Center** (☎ 906-847-6330; www.mackinacparks. com; Huron St).

FATHER MARQUETTE PARK
Right below the fort is this lovely hillside park that serves as a town plaza. You can easily spend an afternoon on the grassy lawn enjoying the cool breezes off the straits and people watching.

BUTTERFLY HOUSE
☎ 906-847-3972; McGulfin St; adult/child $5/2; ⏱ 10am-7pm

Located behind St Anne's Church is this collection of 400 live butterflies, always a favorite stop among children.

ARCH ROCK & FORT HOLMES

A system of roads and trails throughout the interior of the island are used to reach a number of rugged formations that characterize the area. The most famous is Arch Rock on Arch Rock Rd, a natural limestone arch that spans 50ft and rises 146ft above Lake Huron. The best view on the island is reached by enduring the uphill climb along Fort Holmes Rd to Fort Holmes. Sitting on the highest point of the island is the remains of the outpost the British built after retaking the island in the War of 1812.

CYCLING

In either direction Huron St turns into M-185, which skirts the perimeter of the island. This is the only state highway where cars are not allowed. Even so, it's a crowded avenue during the summer with cyclists, in-line skaters and horses. M-185 makes for a 8.4-mile bike ride that is easy and very scenic as you rarely leave the shoreline. You can rent a bike ($16 per half day) from a dozen places on Huron St including **Island Bicycle Livery** (☎ 906-847-6288; ⏰9am-8pm) and **Lakeside/Streetside Bike Rentals** (☎ 906-847-6083; ⏰8:30am-7pm).

CARRIAGE TOURS

Another way to see the island is to hire a horse-drawn taxi or join a carriage tour. You can pick up a taxi at **Father Marquette Park** and negotiate a price depending on the number of people in your party and what you want to see. **Mackinac Island Carriage Tours** (☎ 906-847-3573; adult/child $17/7.50) offers two-hours tours that include Arch Rock, Skull Cave, Grand Hotel and Fort Mackinac. Purchase your tickets from an office next to the information kiosk on Huron St.

SLEEPING

There are few economical lodging options on the island. Most rooms run about $150 per night and during the peak season, weekends are booked months in advance.

GRAND HOTEL

☎ 906-847-3331, 800-33-GRAND; www.grandhotel.com; Grand Ave; d $466-819 includes breakfast & dinner

This is Michigan's most famous hotel. Built in 1887 on a limestone bluff, the Grand Hotel was at the time the world's largest summer hotel, characterized by its 660ft front porch overlooking the Straits of Mackinac. Guests go for the experience of staying in an elegant Victorian hotel where men still must wear a suit and tie and women a dress after 6pm.

ISLAND HOUSE

☎ 906-847-3347, 800-626-6304; www.theislandhouse.com; Huron St, d $160-325

Mackinac's first summer hotel was built in 1852 and has 94 rooms, three suites, an outdoor pool and a fine restaurant with a view of the Straits of Mackinac.

DETOUR: CROSSING THE MIGHTY MAC

One of the most beautiful drives in Michigan is over the **Mackinac Bridge**, a 5-mile stretch of I-75 from Mackinaw City to the edge of St Ignace – unless you're the driver who has to keep an eye on the road. Passengers can gaze at Lake Huron or Lake Michigan, at almost a dozen islands, the Grand Hotel, the shorelines of both the Lower and Upper Peninsulas, and freighters and sailboats below. The toll is $2.50 per vehicle and the scenery is so stunning that one of the most popular events in Michigan is the **Mackinac Bridge Walk** (☎ 906-643-7600; www.mackinacbridge.org). The free event is held every Labor Day, when more than 60,000 people trek across to Mackinaw City and then are bused back to their cars on the north side. It's the only time of the year you are allowed to walk across the Mighty Mac.

East of the bridge on the north shore is **St Ignace** (☎ 800-338-6660; www. stignace.com; 560 N State St; ☼ 9am-5pm Mon-Fri, 10am-2pm Sat), founded in 1671 by Father Jacques Marquette. Within town are hotels, restaurants, a casino and several historical sites and museums including **Marquette Mission Park,** where the famous Jesuit missionary and explorer is buried.

West of the bridge, US 2 skirts the north shore of Lake Michigan for 142 miles until it reaches **Escanaba**, where it heads inland toward **Iron Mountain**. From Escanaba, M-35 hugs the shoreline all the way to Wisconsin. The most scenic section by far is the 50 miles from the bridge to Naubinway, where US 2 passes the best beaches in the Upper Peninsula as well as half dozen rustic state and federal campgrounds. For great beach camping plan on pitching a tent at **Lake Michigan National Forest Campground** (35 sites, $12, 18 miles from the bridge), **Hog Island State Forest Campground** (59 sites, $10; 35 miles from the bridge) or **Big Knob State Forest Campground** (23 sites; $10; 44 miles from the bridge & south on Big Knob Rd). For information on these campgrounds and others stop at the **Hiawatha National Forest Information Center** (☎ 906-643-7900; 1798 US 2; ☼ 8am-4:30pm Mon-Fri) 6 miles west of the bridge.

LA CHANCE COTTAGE
☎ 906-847-3526; Huron St; d $98-105

This 20-room inn is housed in a rambling Victorian mansion that offers simple rooms and shared baths a short walk from the ferries. No TVs or phones, but it's one of the more affordable accommodations downtown.

SMALL POINT B&B
☎ 906-847-3758; Lake Shore Rd; d $75

The island's least expensive place to stay is about a 20-minute walk from the docks, away from the summer crowds. Small Point has a lakeside view and small rooms with shared bathrooms.

EATING

Fudge lovers will find themselves in heaven on Mackinac Island, where they have been making the rich confection since 1889. Today there are more than a dozen shops along Huron St that make fudge daily and use fans to blow the aroma outside to tempt tourists.

FRENCH OUTPOST
☎ 906-847-3772; www.frenchoutpost.com; Cadotte Ave; mains $7-14; ☼ 11am-2am

French Outpost is a cozy restaurant where you can sit within view of the Grand Hotel and enjoy salads or sandwiches with a pint of beer.

FORT MACKINAC TEA ROOM
☎ 906-847-3328; Fort Mackinac; mains $6-15; ☼ 9:30am-6pm

Located in Fort Mackinac, the Tea Room boasts the best view of any restaurant on the island but can only be entered after purchasing a ticket to the fort. Sit outdoors with a sweeping view of the harbor and enjoy salads, sandwiches and historic dishes such as a recipe for corned beef with potatoes and apples that was originally served to officers in the winter of 1883.

WOODS RESTAURANT
☎ 906-847-3331; Stonecliff Rd; mains $16-32; ☼ 5:30-10pm

This Bavarian-style restaurant owned by the Grand Hotel specializes in wild game entrees such as grilled venison chops with red current glaze. It's literally in the woods in the middle of the island, hence the name, and requires a ride in a horse-drawn taxi to reach it.

ASTOR STREET CAFÉ
☎ 906-847-6031; Astor St, mains $6-9; ☼ 11am- 4pm

The Astor is a local favorite that serves affordable subs, burgers, whitefish and spaghetti dinners.

ENTERTAINMENT & SHOPPING

The downtown area, Huron and Market Sts, contains the majority of shops and fudge counters and not coincidentally is where the ferries spill their boatloads of tourists. Among trinket shops selling rubber tomahawks and T-shirts are a surprising number of upscale jewelry and art studios.

At night, the bars and restaurants on the island are a fun mix of tourists, seasonal workers and boaters who just pulled into the harbor. Two particularly lively places that often have entertainment are **Pink Pony Bar & Grill** (☎ 906-847-3341; Huron St; ☼ 10am-2am), in the Chippewa Hotel, and **Horn's Gaslight Bar** (☎ 906-847-6154; Huron St; ☼ 10:30am-2am).

INDEX